No Grazing For Sacred Cows

Tormenting Questions In A Bizarre World

Noel Francisco

CSS Publishing Company, Inc., Lima, Ohio

Library of Congress Cataloging-in-Publication Data

Francisco, Noel, 1923-
    No grazing for sacred cows : tormenting questions in a bizarre world / Noel Francisco.
        p.   cm.
    ISBN 0-7880-1329-7 (pbk.)
    1. Life.   I. Title.
BD431.F672   1999
191—dc21   98-44909
                                                                            CIP

This book is available in the following formats, listed by ISBN:
    0-7880-1329-7   Book
    0-7880-1330-0   Disk
    0-7880-1331-9   Sermon Prep

*This book is dedicated to Barbara — confidante,
reliable critic, companion, friend, wife —
and our children, Lee, Becky, Susan,
and Philip. Each one has
uniquely contributed to
expanded awareness
in the adventure
in living!*

Acknowledgments

Numerous individuals have encouraged me to prepare these writings for publication. Family members, friends, and colleagues have read some or all of the manuscript and shared with me their constructive reactions to what they have read. Rather than risk omitting names of individuals who have contributed their insights for the final edition, I wish to thank everyone who has had a part in this publication. A number of contemporary writers remind us of how all of us are caught up in a web of giving and receiving from our human relationships. Writing and preparing this book has brought this fact clearly home to me.

Table Of Contents

Spiritual Restlessness

Strange World

Some Concluding Grazing

"The man who learns how difficult it is to step outside the intellectual climate of his or any age has taken the first step on the road to emancipation, to world citizenship of a high order." — Loren Eiseley

What price, what price, Leon, must one pay to question the intellectual fashions, the cultural compulsives, the dogmas of one's time?

Introduction

Watch out! The gentle writing you're about to read can bite you!

For the fifty-plus years I have known the author, he has quietly but persistently affirmed democratic and community values. He has quietly but persistently protested against all the external social forces and the inner self-centeredness which threatens those values.

Concerning this book, I can say what Noel Francisco is too modest to say: these are reflections of a modern-day prophet. This book is a kind of sampler of the accumulated wisdom of a lifetime.

Dr. Francisco is a distinguished teacher who combines dispassionate scholarly discipline with passion for human culture and personal compassion for his students.

He and I have sustained a long-running argument:

"Noel, sociology leads you to focus so much on society that you miss the individual."

"Paul, psychology leads you to focus so much on the individual that you ignore the social context."

Well, now in the light of this book I want to say to you, "Noel, you're unmasked! You not only care about the individual but you articulate clearly the dialectic between the person and his/her society. Our running argument is over!"

Seriously, don't let Professor Francisco's gentle style lull you into complacency. Look, and you will find incisive critique, the prophetic bite, on nearly every page. Watch out!

— The Rev. Paul Nicely
   Emeritus Professor of Pastoral Care
   Methodist Theological School in Ohio

Preface

Endeavoring to express our deeply felt thoughts and feelings is difficult for most of us. Many of us go through life bottling up much of our deeper, inner self. It is something like daring really to love another. As numerous writers have pointed out, to do this, to share your most profound self with another, is risky. You are made vulnerable. There is the possibility that what you say and how you express your feelings may at some later time be used against you.

Yet most of us are probably hungry, at least at times, for the opportunity to pour out "our soul" to another. Some writers suggest the need of all of us for a spiritual counselor, guide, director, or confidant. To have someone we greatly respect, someone we feel has deep spiritual roots, someone who can be trusted, someone who will listen, someone to whom we can go and endeavor to communicate our concerns, our misgivings, our longings, and so forth can be a great asset in life. Few of us, though, probably discover the opportunity to cultivate such a relationship.

Although I have been fortunate in having a spouse who serves this purpose in many ways and I have had friends in whom I placed the greatest trust, I have never had any one person that I considered my actual spiritual guide. In a way, then, this group of writings is in the context of trying to express some thoughts that I might share with a spiritual guide or director. "Leon, although the name has special meaning for me, is not any actual person, but stands for an entity that I would consider a spiritual guide.

I hope that what is presented here may be helpful in encouraging individuals to seek a spiritual guide. If no friend or acquaintance can fill this need, then one can, in a journal-like way of writing, construct his or her thought in such a way as to sense one is writing to a spiritual guide.

Some of what I write here may make me vulnerable to others. There are friends and acquaintances who may read what is written here who will have "second thoughts" about me, but it is a risk I am willing to take. (They likely already had their suspicions, anyway!)

A major objective of my teaching was to encourage individuals *to think* about topics considered in the class. Whether or not they might agree with points of view expressed by me was irrelevant as long as they made a genuine effort to think about the subject matter. In a way the same applies to what is set forth here. I don't ask individuals to agree with the questions and thoughts written here. I would just urge some creative thinking about the subjects touched upon, and the questions raised here.

The Human Creature

"The unique place of our species in the order of things is determined not by its animality but by its humanity." — Rene Dubos

— but, Leon, just how thoroughly have we probed our humanity?

What Limits?

We humans possess an aggressive instinct. We are killer apes. Man is a promiscuous creature. By nature, humans are a depraved species. One could keep adding to the assertions of writers about how we humans are born with various traits, Leon. Writers, public speakers, teachers, and people in daily conversation often refer to what they claim are inherent characteristics in us humans. Do they really realize the significance of what they are saying?

Simply stating the matter, are they not compressing us into conditions where certain aspects of our behavior are irremediable? Are they not saying, in so many words, it is written in stone that we have to be aggressive, that we have to be killers, that we have to be promiscuous, that we have to be treacherous or whatever particular trait is being described as a part of our biological nature?

Should we not be disturbed by this kind of writing and thinking, Leon?* Does it not suggest a kind of defeatist attitude that since humans are born with such and such traits, there is really nothing that can be done about our behavior? These perspectives also suggest what I suspect are really distortions. A much broader range of scholarship and research on the subject of human behavior is omitted by such writing and thought.

Well do I remember some years ago the President of the American Psychological Association saying that probably the major discovery in the behavioral sciences, which might be comparable to some of the major discoveries in the physical sciences, is the *plasticity* of human behavior. Granted we are biological creatures and that there are limits to what our biological inheritance can allow us to do, within those limits there is a broad range of behavior in which we humans can engage.

Leon, I don't believe many of us very seriously apply the belief that specific traits in us are incapable of some modification. For instance, conscientious parents do not believe their young children are cast in some kind of die that they can do nothing about.

Do they not endeavor to guide and direct their children in the kind of behavioral traits they hope they will develop?

I know there is a great deal of pessimism around today. We are shaken by the terrible human slaughter that has been taking place during this twentieth century. One would have to be ignorant of a large part of the news being reported not to be aware of the savagery and cruelty of many of our fellow humans. But, Leon, I almost suspect that it is weary souls who are concluding that this kind of behavior is totally a reflection of our genes. Are they not weary of trying to see beyond our human foibles and recognize more admirable characteristics and potentials that we also possess?

Furthermore, I wonder, if there is something suspect about us humans, is it not our appetite for sensational news? And human violence is sensational to write about. Apparently, it is not exciting to tell about how altruistic humans can be, is it, Leon? How humans can dedicate their lives to fostering good will and mutual aid among one another is dull, isn't it? Or is it? C. Wright Mills once wrote that we really don't know what the limits of human behavior are for "bad" or "good." I would like to be inspired to do all that I can do to push those limits for the good in us! There might even be something sensational and exciting to report here!

---

*True, much research is being done about genetic influences on us, and much of this research holds promise for treatment of our human disorders. Responsible, careful scientific research in genetics is not what disturbs me, Leon. Rather it is the popular sensational writing and speaking about human behavior which makes sweeping claims about how we humans are imprisoned and immobilized by our "inherited nature."

Flawed Humans?

I'm a far more suggestible individual, Leon, than I would like to admit. If people significant to me suggest that I am a brilliant person, I tend to think that maybe I am more intelligent than I give myself credit for being. If they indicate to me that I am a sharp-appearing man, I can look in the mirror and see an image of myself that is not so bad to look at after all. If they convey to me that I am a disorganized professor, I become uncomfortable with my careless manner of keeping my books, papers, and files. If they view me as an aloof individual, I begin to worry about how well I relate to others. And so on I could go. I am a very suggestible human.

There is a doctrine and perspective related to this matter of suggestibility that is a pervasive and long-established emphasis in our cultural heritage. A dominant theme in our Western religious heritage projects upon us humans that we are imperfect, selfish, flawed creatures. We are sinners; something about the core of our being is tainted. By our very nature, according to this tradition, we are a species that suffers from an inherent, condemnatory, evil streak that limits us and contributes to our suffering and pain.

Often this influence in our culture has affected how I look at myself. I don't have to look far to see that I am a sinner; often I fail to live up to ideals and values that I strive to uphold. Sometimes, Leon, this condition makes me feel downright miserable about myself. Are not many others who have been raised in our environment affected in similar ways? Have not many of us been conditioned to view ourselves as imperfect, inadequate, wretched beings as a result of these contemporary views projected upon our thinking by religious, political, and educational leaders? One even wonders, Leon, if writers like Matthew Fox may not have a point when they write that such views make it possible for these leaders more easily to control us? Many of these leaders have their own formula or remedy for rescuing us from this flawed state of existence! We, in our weakened condition, are to follow them.

17

If we come to think of ourselves in this manner, how healthy is it for us, Leon? Do we ever entirely shake this view of ourselves as somehow inherently evil-inclined creatures? At an early age of suggestibility, we have absorbed these views that we are unruly, naughty, selfish, sinful creations. Many of us, consequently, don't have a very high estimation of ourselves or of the species of which we are a part.

I would certainly acknowledge that I find it difficult to locate reliable evidence or sound arguments that we humans are perfect creatures. For one thing, I don't know what perfect would be. Then, too, I know only too well that I often behave in ways that fall far short of what I believe to be more wholesome and praiseworthy conduct. I am sure that I, like others around me, am not nearly as good as I could be. But I question this suggestion that my cultural heritage has thrust upon me, that this condition of not being as good as I could be is the result of some inborn, imperfect, flawed characteristic peculiar to us humans.

What if we could look upon ourselves, Leon, in a more neutral manner? What if we could view ourselves as creatures with much untapped potentiality? What, with this more neutral perspective, if we could recognize that we have much potential for either good or bad? What if we could sense that this potential can be directed in an almost infinite variety of ways that can benefit ourselves and others? If we could discard any kind of thinking that this potential in and of itself is flawed, that we are not restrained from birth on by an irremediable defect, what might be the freeing, emancipating effect? What might repeated suggestions of our potential for realizing more good in our personalities do for our self-images?

Add to this kind of thought a belief that there is a spark of divinity in each of us, and we have a condition, it seems to me, that contains powerful possibilities for creating more good in our world. Is not the suggestion of divine kinship far more conducive to our well-being than thinking of ourselves as basically evil, sinful creatures? I, for one, would prefer to look in the mirror and see an image there of one who possesses a potential for activating much more good by the very being I am, than to see in the mirror a questionable, blemished, marred creature that may be doomed to failure because of what it is.

The more I think about it, Leon, the more I would wish to avoid passing on to the present or future generations any kind of suggestion that they are born flawed creatures. I wonder if this view, in the many forms it takes, may not be an infliction upon us that is really unnecessary. Would that we could open our eyes more clearly and quicken our understanding more fully of what may be contributing to unnecessary restraints on us humans for realizing more good in our lives.

Questioning

A plaque showing a young boy curiously, questioningly bent over examining an object on a beach with a quote at the top, "The important thing is not to stop questioning," by Albert Einstein, has hung on my study wall for many years. Earlier in my teaching career, Leon, I did not realize the importance of this message. Now I wonder if it doesn't come close to arriving at the heart of human vitality? Would it be going too far to say that a really alive person is a questioning individual?

For much of my teaching career, I did not really encourage my students to raise questions. I wanted to provide them with answers and I fear I expected them to accept the answers I gave them and not question them. If members of my classes had asked many searching questions during the early years of my teaching, I suspect I would have felt threatened. I was, after all, a new Ph.D. and I was supposed to be well informed in my field of study. Why would anyone be brazen enough to question what I was teaching!

This point of view on my part changed in the latter years of my classroom procedures. I often commenced classes at the beginning of a term encouraging members to formulate and ask what they considered to be important questions related to the subjects we were studying. Sometimes on an examination the students would be asked to formulate and write down what they considered to be four or five of the most important questions related to the particular subject of the course. Some students responded well to this kind of teaching, but many were confused and uncomfortable. They were accustomed to memorizing data and information given to them by their teachers and then poll-parrot back on their examinations what they had copied in class.

Isn't this a widespread tendency, Leon, for adults to relinquish deep, searching, questioning attitudes? We are taught not just to refrain from questioning our teachers, but also our parents, our work supervisors, our priests and clergy, our elected political leaders, and our community leaders. Don't most individuals in positions of leadership feel insecure when followers question their policies and decisions? In many instances is not questioning viewed as some kind of devious behavior?

For many of us to view important areas of life as open to serious questioning, furthermore, is unsettling for us. We want answers to the crucial issues of life. We don't like uncertainty, do we? And don't we seek those clergy, teachers, political leaders, and others who provide us with the answers? The availability of such leaders is usually not difficult to find! Some of us may go so far in our entrusting our lives to these leaders that we die with them in mass suicidal situations. Recent events with some cultist groups are disturbing illustrations of this tendency. Open encouragement of questioning is discouraged if not outright forbidden in many groups in which we may participate.

When our questioning tendencies are stifled, don't we humans lose something vital and unique in our living? Does not a kind of intellectual and spiritual atrophy occur with us? What seems as such a natural, inquisitive, questioning tendency of early childhood we seem to lose as we settle into the grooves of adulthood. If something like this is what happens to many of us, are we not a species to be pitied? Would you say, Leon, that maybe the cosmic powers are disappointed with many of us? Perhaps they thought with the human experiment something noble and extremely creative was under way. But has something gone wrong along the way whereby we have abandoned our birthright? Uncomfortably, I fear, we teachers may bear much of the responsibility for this.

A Tragic Species?

Financial advisors caution people about putting all their investments in one source and many individuals heed what they say. But when it comes to the most profound "securities" in our lives, don't many of us ignore this advice? Don't we, Leon, all too often put our ultimate sense of security in our job, our home, our financial reserves, our spouse, our family, our career, or some other more or less tangible person or asset? When something removes these ultimate securities are we not left devastated?

We humans do need some kind of a sense of security, don't we? Gnawing away at us, more than probably most of us realize, is this deep-seated awareness that we are mortal creatures. This knowledge, even though we may be able to keep it out of our consciousness most of the time, nevertheless fuels our search for security. In fact, this drive for security is probably much more powerful, isn't it, than the much-publicized desire for freedom that especially our political leaders keep championing with their varied rhetoric? Is not much of the desperate behavior we humans experience related to the anxieties that arise from the inner disquietude that this mortality awareness arouses in us? Do we not endeavor to master these anxieties by seeking offsetting securities, only still to harbor an uneasiness that these "ultimate securities" are inadequate when threatened?

Are we not foolish, Leon, in how we often choose our source of "ultimate security"? Now it is somewhat more obvious, at least to some of us, the futility that is present in endeavoring to think we can gain security by the ownership and possession of objects like new automobiles, houses, expensive recreational equipment, and so forth. We perceive the deception in advertising that security is to be found in the purchase of these commodities. A close look at these tangible objects as important sources of security reveals how fleeting, disposable, and temporary they are.

But other ways in which we may try to find security may not be so obvious. We may develop and experience a deep, abiding love in our spouse, in a friend, or in our family. We may be unaware of how much our sense of security is tied up with these loved ones. Then when an illness or accident occurs we are shaken by the realization that even these treasured, valued relationships fall short in providing any ultimate security.

What kind of a bind are we humans placed in, Leon? We crave security but are unable to find any ultimate source for relieving this drive. Is some kind of giant hoax being played upon us by the universe? Are we to experience one disillusionment after another as the varied bases of our securities disclose their inadequacies?

We do have in our heritage guidelines here that can help us, don't we, Leon? Don't all the great religious traditions have something to say about this subject? In our own Judeo-Christian heritage we are cautioned against placing too much confidence in "the things of this world." We are dramatically reminded of the folly of piling up treasures where moth and rust eventually creep in and destroy. But we learn these lessons slowly and painfully.

Just because we are mortal creatures we are not left in complete despair, though, are we? Does not our religious heritage assure us with repeated emphases that human life is not confined by what we can perceive with our sensual capacities? In this heritage is there not a sobering and pervasive theme that our lives are more than just a fleeting bubble bounded by time and space? Are we not directed towards threads of eternity that infuse our lives? In those moments when we may catch glimpses of this theme in our and others' lives, is it not something like the sun suddenly breaking through an overcast sky and overwhelming us with a grandeur that shatters the anxieties that have tormented us?

Leon, I just don't believe we are a tragic species. There is a quality about us humans and our ties with "something" in this universe that bespeaks a relationship and realization that we have barely begun to understand. *We do need*, though, more instruction in contemporary terms and language we can understand. We need much enlightenment here.

No doubt, it seems we do have an agonizing assignment before us. We have to learn to give up our prized possessions, our sources of security, whatever they may be, for they all fail in the long run in giving us that security that we want. But in saying we have to learn to give them up, are we not affirming that we are giving them up for something far more worthy of our commitment than what we have had? We don't have to be fools, Leon. It may be old-fashioned to say so, but I don't care; I know there is a spark of divinity in all of us. And that spark can transform our anxious lives!

Whistling In The Dark

There have been some humorous eye-catching drawings made of boys walking past a cemetery after dark, whistling as they hastily passed this menacing patch of landscape. But, Leon, it is not only boys who whistle in the dark when they are apprehensive, but all of us do this at times, don't we? Are we not inclined to don a false facade of bravery when we encounter life-threatening situations?

Could it be that many of us endeavor to go through life spending much of the time engaged in what amounts to whistling in the dark? Don't we try to act as though we are unaffected by the deeper issues of our humanity? Are we not products of a culture which camouflages the reality that we are mortal beings? Don't we almost feel that to acknowledge our mortality is somehow a sign of weakness? In some circles is it not almost a censored subject to consider that busy, active, important executive branch individuals are humans that can become sick, can be involved in accidents, can die just like anyone else? Are some of us absorbed in a charade in which we act as if we shall live forever? Leon, this kind of deceptive behavior is distressing!

Very likely some of us are influenced by those currents in our culture that are still rebelling against the old hellfire and damnation religions of the past. We have recoiled from the efforts of theatrical clergy dangling us over the pits of hell on the one hand and with the other holding out the promise of some gilded heaven. Such psychological manipulation has appeared to us as something juvenile. Consequently, have we glossed over the deeper, basic, disturbing questions of human experience?

What happens to us, then, Leon, when we are jarred into the realization of how mortal we are? I fear it is a real shock for many of us. We just are not prepared for coping with these inevitable occurrences in our lives.

Is there not a real tragedy here? At a late moment in life, do we not frantically seek some source that can relieve us of our fears in these distressing moments? Does this not raise the question of what is the most important relationship to be aware of and to culti-vate, that we have ignored and neglected? Is it not our relation-ship with God? One may wish to use other names to designate the awareness of a Power or Force that we come to realize surpasses the limits of our human mortality, but the actual name of reference does not seem crucial. Here is a relationship that can be the most personal of all relationships, the most reassuring of all relation-ships, the most comforting of all relationships, the most depend-able of all relationships — and we disregard it! We humans don't really have to whistle in the dark, do we, Leon?

Family Strengths

"Many people think enough of their mates to love them; yet trusting is a greater compliment than loving. (As Job trusted in God even through pain, anger, and resentment.)"
— Sydney J. Harris

Leon, does it not seem that the major cultural patterns of today continually erode trust among us?

Insights

The classes never did turn out as I would have liked. I am talking, Leon, about the many Marriage and Family classes that I taught. Here was one of the most important and challenging subjects a teacher could have the opportunity to teach; yet the classes never did suit me. Although I endeavored to work plenty of humor into the classes, maybe there was not enough. Maybe the complaint of one student that what was wrong with these classes was that they did not include a laboratory with them had some merit. Maybe my expectations were just too high, Leon.

Anyway, if students did not obtain the insights that I hoped they would about marriage and family life, at least I did! I guess the old saying that a teacher learns from his teaching more than anyone else was true with me. Reflecting upon these classes, some of the most important insights that I recall were the following:

Many marriages in American culture today are not successful and meaningful unless the partners develop the ability to communicate and share their feelings. Women, and I think men too, look for companionship in marriage, and meaningful companionship cannot be experienced unless there is mutual communication and sharing of each other's real feelings and emotions. Unfortunately, many American men appear poorly trained for such communication.

In turn, such sharing requires empathy. This ability to enter into the situations and life of one's spouse and sense and feel how he or she is experiencing the particular situations in which the other is living at the moment seems crucial, Leon, for contemporary marriages. There are individuals who just seem to be unable to possess and express empathy with others; such individuals, I fear, are going to have marital difficulties. I don't know if individuals are born with this ability to have empathy for others or if it is a trait one develops. I have had several lively discussions with colleagues on this point. Whatever may be involved here, to possess and express empathy is extremely important to marriage.

Really implied in what has been said is the practice of kindness. I never did run across much resource material on this subject as I prepared my lectures, but it does seem very important in marriages today. For some reason, many marriages appear to have little kindness present in them. It has always baffled me how two human individuals in the ties of marriage can show so little kindness for one another. Many individuals can show much more kindness toward their pet dog or cat than they can toward their spouse. Too many marriages today could be characterized as being brutal. The individuals constituting the marriage have not yet been civilized, maybe, Leon?

Commitment is another essential requirement in contemporary marriages. And commitment appears to be a factor that many of us for some reason are really reluctant to make. Probably our highly mobile, transitory kind of living has something to do with this. Changes about us are so rapid and impact our lives in so many ways that to commit ourselves to a place, to a group, or to an individual is strange and uncomfortable for us. But with all the demands made upon marriages and families today, unless there is a strong commitment to the marriage, to the relationship that the marriage essentially is, most marriages will not withstand the almost inevitable difficulties that couples will sooner or later experience.

Contemporary marriages are founded on a fragile base compared with marriages of a few generations ago. There is not the societal and institutional propping up of marriages that our recent ancestors had behind their marriages. As we Americans gradually began to make love the ultimate basis for marriage, a quite different environment emerged for supporting marriages. Now marriage was dependent upon an unpredictable emotional state that was subject to many individual mood swings. What individuals considered the love element in their marriage could be quite unstable and transitory. Marriage today is, therefore, a difficult undertaking in many ways. Here is another reason, Leon, for the emphasis upon commitment, isn't it?

These reflections make me wonder if writers like Joseph Campbell may not sense the ultimate insight here into the subject of marriage when they emphasize that marriage, to be a real, true, *bona fide* marriage, requires a lifetime commitment, which means making the marriage relationship a prime concern. Do you agree, Leon? I think perhaps I do. But these insights are very difficult to convey to others, aren't they?

Vulnerable

The small boy had hit his head sharply on the corner of a table and he fought back the tears. His father nearby was ready to comfort him, but allowed him to struggle to keep his composure. Even a young boy must not show his emotions too easily. He was learning, wasn't he, Leon, to keep his feelings guarded? Isn't this how we are reared, especially boys, in our culture?

What may such training do to us as we become adults, Leon? There are scholars who say that it contributes to many of us males being inadequate marriage partners. We don't know how to communicate on a meaningful emotional level with our spouses. Hence the deeper love that we might experience with our wives fails to develop as we restrain our emotions.

Is what is involved here a part of a larger problem? Because of how we are raised, are we humans fearful of adventuring into greater rapport with others? Do we decrease the meaning of many of our human encounters by sterile emotional communication?

Are those professionals correct who maintain that to love others requires making ourselves more vulnerable to them? No doubt, it seems to me, Leon, to open up to others — to communicate how you really feel about persons, unreservedly to state how you regard the world about you, to express what are your "gut feelings," to tell others what you are thinking at the moment — all this involves risks that many of us are unwilling to take. To reveal that you have tender feelings, that you have insecurities, that you harbor disturbing thoughts, that you have entertained obscene daydreams, that you are not nearly as certain of yourself as you try to appear, that you really do long to be loved and to be understood — such revelations do not come easily for most of us. To let others know that we have such feelings and thoughts provides information to be used against us by anyone who may wish to betray our trust. As we say sometimes, we can get our fingers burnt in opening up to others.

Yet, Leon, can we really experience the richness and fullness of life if we blindly continue to censor our urges to communicate more thoroughly with others? What do we really gain in holding back? If the truth were really known, Leon, are not many of us settling for anemic lives? For us males especially, one could almost cry out and plead that we be prodded into discarding the imprisoned shells into which we have been forced and which emotionally impoverish us!

It takes courage to love, doesn't it, Leon? Isn't love opening our locked doors of emotional restraint and experiencing the adventure of sharing our deepest feelings and longings? Isn't love expressing our compassion, our identification with others, and discovering our common humanity? Isn't love allowing the full potential of our humaneness to flourish?

So Thankful

I looked over at her sitting on the car seat beside me. She was dozing at the moment, but she had been watching, as she has many times, for any threats that might endanger our safety as we drove along.

Right now her posture reminded me of the loyal, constant, reliable companion she had been for over forty years. She was beautiful as she sat there. I would have liked to have taken her in my arms and, with full communicative ability on my part, told her how much I appreciated her, how much I enjoyed her company, how much I treasured the many experiences we had been privileged to share, how much I really loved her.

Leon, I'm a lucky man to have her as companion, helpmate, consoler, mutual adventurer, wife! Early in our marriage we used to say to one another, "Life is adventurous." And it has been. It has been for us. To a large extent it has been so because we have been able to share so many varied, exciting moments. At times, in rather grim or trying moments, we have broken the solemnity of the occasion by reminding the other "that life is adventurous" and we would be able to laugh and shatter the gravity that had checked us. What a balanced, rejuvenating spirit she has provided for our marriage!

Do many individuals get to experience this kind of marriage, this kind of marvelous relationship? Is it true, Leon, that many of our contemporaries are short-changing themselves and their spouses by parting ways over minor obstacles that appear to interfere with their personal pleasures? Is it only sensual attachments that are temporarily binding many couples? Are they failing to develop the patience, understanding, kindness, and zest that builds enduring marriages?

Gosh, Leon, it seems they are missing a lot. With whom are they going to share long-held memories as they enter the "golden years"? Who will help them recall names, places, events that elude momentary recall? Who will be there to experience the reliving of exciting moments of valued happenings of the distant past? Who will they feel close enough to that, based on years of confidence-building, they can say and act as they really feel?

Leon, thanks for my tried and trusted companion. The love for her just keeps growing and maturing in overwhelming ways! What more can I say?

Communication

Many of us fathers, Leon, when we have young sons and daughters, expect our communication with our sons will be easier as they grow up than it will be with our daughters. But in my case, this has not seemed to be true. Our oldest son, when he was a young boy, was a great pleasure to have accompany me various places. There was the making of a companionship that I greatly looked forward to. As he was to become older, I projected ready communication with him on subjects ranging from daily events to profound philosophical topics. Something happened along the way, Leon!

He had barely entered the adolescent years when his independent tendencies became more and more obvious. Our culture with its emphasis upon independence was readily being absorbed by our son. Adolescent peer relationships further undermined the promising companionship we had experienced when he was younger. Communication was becoming more infrequent and mildly strained as the months and years accumulated. At times I would casually toss out ideas that I hoped would bring some response from him, only to find a wall of silence greeting me. I had not expected this. Even though I was supposed to be a professional with some advanced knowledge of what to anticipate in situations like this, I was not prepared for what I was experiencing with my own son.

I wondered, Leon, if I was somehow failing as a father. If I had tried and kept endeavoring to keep the lines of communication open with him, could I not expect free and open sharing of thoughts and reactions to what he was experiencing? But this was not happening. Was I failing? I guess I shall never know.

Consequently, I have complained that I missed and regretted the full communication with our son that I had counted on when he was a child. Then, Barbara has reminded me that there are other modes of communication than spoken, written means. And I begin to recall moments when Lee and I had worked together or gone someplace and, although few words were spoken, more of an exchange of feelings and thoughts had occurred during such moments than I had realized at the time. There was a feeling of mutual trust, respect for our differences, admiration for our individual achievements and abilities, satisfaction of being in each other's company. Don't moments like these, when non-verbalized feelings and attitudes are shared, communicate maybe much more than clumsily expressed spoken words? Probably so, don't you think?

It is easy, so writers tell us, Leon, for many of us American fathers to develop quite easily a sense of guilt about how we have failed to be the fathers we had hoped to be. I certainly have gone this route numerous times as my children were growing up. Yet perhaps some of us have been too hard on ourselves. Undetected, there may have been significant channels of understanding and good will between a father and his children. It seems more often the case that we are alerted to the weaknesses and even pathologies that may develop in father-son, parent-child relationships than we are of existing strengths in those relationships.

I really appreciate my son Lee. He doesn't occupy the White House; he is not a prominent professional; he isn't an outstanding athlete; he isn't a renowned scholar. He is just a good, solid citizen, a caring father himself, and an individual whose wholesome company is appreciated. I am proud of him. Something worthwhile, I believe, Leon, has been communicated between us!

A Salute

There she walks carefree into the store. No sign of self-consciousness on her part about being only a matter of days away from giving birth to her first child. She is sharply dressed in a maternity jump outfit. A certain radiance seems to emanate from her. She is a striking person, Leon. No doubt about it — even if I am looking through the eyes of a proud father.

This expectant child is very special to Becky and Denny. As is common now with working couples, they have postponed having a child until rather late in the child-bearing years. After much thought on the subject, they decided to become parents. It takes a lot of courage these days deliberately to make this kind of decision. To bring new human life in to this confusing, complex, fast-paced world really takes courage and foresight.

I am reminded, Leon, of how Barbara and I hesitated to make possible the conception of our first child. The first test hydrogen bomb had just been detonated. Did we want to bring a child into this kind of precarious world? We thought of brave, wise, prophetic individuals of the past* who, in the face of what appeared as impending tragedies, nevertheless proceeded to live and plan as though life would continue in a normal fashion. We had this first child and later two more were born into our family. We don't regret, by any means whatsoever, bringing this new life into our world. But it does take courage knowingly to have children with the possible suffering little ones might have to experience. One shudders to think what the mothers and fathers of little children have been through in recent years in places like Bosnia, Rwanda, and Cambodia. What fears, anxieties, and grief have raged through their minds.

Yes, Leon, these children of ours, like Barbara and I a generation ago, want to give birth to new life — even in the face of the uncertainties the future holds. God willing, I know, Leon, that they will exert all the efforts they can to provide a creative, wholesome, and exemplary home for this child. It is sobering to see the kind of responsibility they are willing to assume!   I salute them!

---

*One thinks here of prophets such as Jeremiah, who purchased land even though he prophesied of the coming doom of his country. (Jeremiah 32)

An Autonomous Person

On the inside cover of a Sigurd Olson book which she gave me for my sixtieth birthday, she wrote, "As Sigurd Olson is a shining light to northern Minnesota, so is my father to me." Who could help but have affectionate thoughts toward a daughter who wrote remarks like this? But more than the appreciation of a father for a daughter who expresses her love so forthrightly is the awareness of the sensitive, thoughtful, and caring person this daughter is.

Truly, Leon, she is a remarkably sensitive, thoughtful, and caring person. Furthermore, a sense of positive humor balances situations for her and her family that might tend otherwise to become extremely grave and solemn. She has a way of telling about incidents in her family life that projects her husband and young daughters in a delightfully human, down-to-earth fashion. She generates warmth, comfort, and good will when she is present in a group. Simply put, whenever she is around, one just feels better for having been in her presence.

In many ways she can give the appearance of possessing a child-like naiveté, but when you learn to know her better, you soon begin to realize such a characterization is misleading. Underneath this simplicity is an intelligent individual who has an enlightened grasp of the world in which we live. She does not brandish, though, her intellectual powers, and only in situations where wise heads are needed are her keen, understanding abilities more explicitly displayed.

One would think that with the formal education she has and the keen mind that she possesses, she would be unsuited for playing the role of homemaker. Many would say that she is too modern a person to be content with what many view as a confining life. But not Sue. Most of the time she delights in the opportunities to share in the experiences of her husband and daughters. Her face especially lights up when she relates family incidents; she describes such occurrences as though a major part of the time in their family is one lively affair. And I think it is much of the time, Leon!

It is reassuring to observe that not all of our children's generation have to try to get on the latest fashion trains and present pictures of individuals absorbed with discarding much of the past and its values. She has chosen the kind of lifestyle she is living and there are no indications she is sorry about her choice. She comes close, Leon, to being that kind of autonomous personality that David Riesman wrote about more than a generation ago. She ignores, if she chooses to do so, what her contemporaries endeavor to impose upon others. Her values, her likes and dislikes, her aspirations, and her method of relating to others are of her choosing. She can accept or reject the modes of living of her peers. She is her own person. There is plenty of room for individuals like this, isn't there, in our world today?

Adoption

Why did we do it, Leon? There is no easy answer. Maybe it was not the thing to do. But we really wanted to. We had thought about the matter for a number of years. We had given birth to three children and we wanted to expand our family. Yet we were hesitant with all the population pressures on our planet to give birth to any more children. Then, too, in our involvement in previous social service work, we had witnessed numerous children being sent to state institutions, when what they needed were more normal home environments in which to grow. We were idealistic, I know, but we hoped maybe we could provide a nurturing home for some child that might otherwise be deprived of such an opportunity.

So we adopted Philip. We don't regret what we did. We do know we could have done better as adoptive parents. But we tried. Yes, Leon, we know we even adopted across what we humans refer to as racial lines. Many contemporaries consider this foolish action. We wanted to be color-blind and we wanted to raise this fourth child in a color-blind environment. Did we succeed? Partially, I think. But in a race-conscious world and society, such an objective probably cannot fully be achieved in this period of human history.

We loved this child. He was really a special child to us. Maybe the quality of love for him was not quite of the same kind as for our other children. We certainly didn't want this love to be any less for him. True, later on there were strains and misunderstandings in our relationships. But does family life ever continue indefinitely on a smooth course? Mutual efforts toward reconciliation and renewed communication have helped to heal much. Leon, we hope that there have been creative seeds planted in the lives of all of our children that will make this experience a definitely positive one for each of them. And we do love Philip for the person he is.

Using Our Children

Jim* was elected president of his class and was on the honor roll both semesters. He was selected as a member of the all-state football team and received the local service club scholarship for a summer of study in Europe. Janice* is in her second year in college and won first place in the regional collegiate violin competition last fall. She was on the honor roll for first-year students and will be accompanying her string quartet to England this spring. The list of accomplishments is frequently much longer than this when news of friends' families is received on some of our Christmas cards. For some parents, Christmas notes are a time to publicize the achievements and successes of their children.

This would not be just simple bragging, would it, Leon? Are those friends who receive such messages supposed to compare the records of their friends' children with their own children and see how one's own children stack up with the competition? Does a kind of scorekeeping proceed from year to year to see whose children are coming out on top? What kind of subtle (often not very subtle) competition may exist with many of us Americans? Has our emphasis upon being a competitive people gone so far that we now *use* our children to compete with one another, and, by some strange quirk, we as parents experience some sense of winning over other parents by the accomplishments of our children? May there be forms of exploitation present here that we refuse to recognize?

Leon, did I miss the boat somewhere along the way here? I have always been reluctant to list the achievements of our children in our holiday messages. Is there something mentally and spiritually unhealthy in pressuring our children to more and more successes? I have probably, as a father, overreacted and failed to encourage our children to exert themselves more toward achievements that would have brought public recognition. But I must confess I do not feel remorseful that I may have failed some here, for

43

somehow there is a false ring in much of this competition into which we parents shove our children. Are there not enough pressures in our world that our children are going to encounter without us parents unduly complicating their lives? Can't we as parents restrain ourselves and cease using our children to expand our egos through them?

When our children were younger, we did endeavor to encourage certain guiding principles in their lives to help them more and more make their own decisions. It was painful at times to sit back and see them fail to continue certain pursuits at which they could have been more successful. I was told, for instance, by his junior high music instructor that our son had considerable musical ability with the instrument he played but that he did not practice enough. When he decided to abandon playing this instrument, I hated to see him make this decision. But what is there to gain in forcing our children to engage in such activities as these if they really are not interested in them?

We wanted our children as they were growing up to be themselves. What do I mean by this? I guess I would say that we hoped our children would be, as much as possible, what *they* wanted to be. As they grew older and important decisions confronted them, we hoped they would sense, there in the background, that we were always available to provide guidance and direction if consulted. In this framework, we did endeavor to create a setting in which we hoped they could be joyful, caring, loving individuals. Were we too far off track here? I hope not!

———————————

*fictitious names

An Impossible Wish

Leon, how I would like to spare my children and loved ones much of the unnecessary pain and folly we humans experience. We are such gullible people and unprotestingly accept the goals for our living that those about us foist upon us. During this century the advertising business has expanded into all facets of our lives and intensifies and sanctifies our acceptance and acquisition of what we are told is worthwhile. Buy, consume, enjoy, discard, and buy, consume, enjoy, and discard and on *ad infinitum* the practice continues. We are led to believe that this "American Dream" is the ultimate goal to be achieved. Yet, in the final run, this dream turns out to be a red herring. Late in our lives we awaken to the shallow, superficial lives we have led and sense that we have seldom, if ever, experienced life at its deeper levels.

Many of us appear to skim over opportunities for experiencing the greater depths of life. Like the drama *Our Town* we awaken too late and realize how we have missed the many chances to communicate meaningfully with our loved ones. Often we have even failed to tell them in recognizable ways how much we love them. We just take our love for each other for granted. Similarly we do the same with the loyalty, respect, courtesies, cooperation, and kindness they daily share with us.

Seldom, if ever, do we express and share our subterranean feelings and thoughts. Death, possible misfortunes, failing health, misgivings about our abilities to be "successful," daydreams, ambitions, temptations, jealousies, and so forth are jailed within us. Our society and culture glosses over spontaneous conversation on these universal feelings and thoughts and substitutes pictures of comfortable, carefree, fun living. We are discouraged from expressing in the company of loved ones those very thoughts that stir us most intensely.

If only the insights and understanding that seem to come with accumulated years could be more effectively communicated and shared with our children and other loved ones, how different our lives could be. We would like to spare them the absurdities, the errors, the disillusionments we have made. We all have so much to learn; yet it seems to take most of a lifetime before we begin really to comprehend even a few of the basic, living truths that have arisen out of the pooled experiences of humanity. I guess it is an impossible wish, Leon, to want to save our children and loved ones from the agonies, errors, and wasted moments we have finally recognized in our own lives. But it does hurt to see them repeating our same mistakes. Is this another one of the generational distresses of being a parent?

A Gratifying Moment

"What is your brother doing these days?" "Oh, he's a successful accountant out West." "How did your nephew come out in that sales campaign he was involved with down in Tennessee?" "That was a great success. He was able to steer his company into number one in sales for the entire Southern region."

Leon, are we Americans preoccupied with success? If one were to listen in on many conversations, one could easily conclude that we are. Many of us parents urge our children on to be successful early in their lives. We want them to be successful in school. We want them to be successful in athletics. We want them to be successful in finding a charming mate. We want them to be successful in their jobs. We want them to be successful in making large sums of money. Not to be successful is interpreted automatically as being a failure.

How thoroughly, how deeply, how critically, do most people, though, inquire into what we mean by success? At its core, does it not mean, to most Americans, making a lot of money? Does it mean obtaining high praise and recognition? Does it mean becoming "number one" in some kind of competition? No doubt it has varied meanings when analyzed. But whatever the meaning, can one upon close inspection fail to observe that vanity is associated with success? Does not the drive for success encourage the development of vane individuals?

The well-known Catholic writer Thomas Merton wrote that if he had a message to any of his contemporaries it was one thing: "Be anything you like, be madmen, drunks, and bastards of every shape and form, but at all costs avoid one thing: *success*." * Merton sensed something very demeaning to humans about the way we publicize success, did he not, Leon? Would not scholars with spiritual insights agree with Merton? I tend to think they would.

Never will I forget, Leon, the day my son made an unexpected visit to my campus office. Seldom did he stop by my office. When he did, I knew something important was on his mind. He had been working a number of months for a regional company and was being groomed to assume a managerial position. His company had been flying him to various midwestern cities to become acquainted with its operations. He was making the most money he had ever made. His economic future looked quite bright. Success was definitely within his reach.

Yet I thought I had sensed some thinly-concealed discontent on his part with his work. After some light conversation in my office, my son said, "Dad, I'm going to quit my job. All that the people in charge of the company have on their mind is making money and more money. Nothing else really matters to them."

In some ways I was not surprised with what he said. Yet, as a typical father, I was concerned with the effects that his resignation would have for him and his family. Good jobs then were beginning to become more scarce and, from all I had observed and read, they would become even more scarce in the months ahead. I feared some of the deprivation he and his family might experience.

Yet, Leon, those moments with my son in my campus office were among the most gratifying moments that I have had in recent years. My son saw through the superficiality of much of what we Americans associate with success. He had the wisdom and courage to reject boarding the "success treadmill"! Yes, I was proud of my son. I believe he understood something of what Merton was writing. He saw, among other things, that there is much more to life than just making money! Amen!

----

*Merton, Thomas, *Love and Living*, edited by Naomi Burton Stone and Brother Patrick Hart (New York: Bantam Books, 1979), p. 10.

Secularization?

The family Christmas gathering has come and gone —

Children and grandchildren have hurried back to their homes —

Many were the gifts opened; grandchildren tore into one package after another.

Scarcely had they glanced at the contents of one gift until they were searching for others to rip open.

Excitement, anticipation, clamor, commotion, confusion ruled the event.

It was a lively, stimulating time.

But yet, but yet, Leon, something was missing.

For many years when my father was a part of the Christmas circle —

Before gifts were opened, he read the Gospel Christmas Story and offered prayer.

This became a tradition.

We were impatient to hurry to the gifts; the few moments of scripture reading and prayer delayed the rush to the gifts —

Yet a tone was set for the gathering and a link with ageless tradition was sensed.

I tried, Leon, to continue this observance in our family —

Written prayers, sometimes agonizingly prepared to include meaningful, relevant thoughts, were read in unison to open our gift exchanges.

This year, in one of the children's homes, no mention was made of retaining this observance.

It was off to glory in the products of the marketplace.

Is our family typical, Leon?

Does a link with our religious past mean nothing to us anymore?

Have we become completely secularized?

Are we joining that throng of seemingly drifting, rootless, anomic creatures who live for the moment?

Leon, what have I helped to sire here?

Much responsibility rests with me; have I failed to provide spiritual guidance to my loved ones?

I hope I am misinterpreting the event, Leon.

But I am not so sure I have.

An Extremely Difficult Adjustment

Control and supervision of our lives from our children? Never, many of us aging parents would probably say! Yet as we advance in years this possibility, or a close proximity to it, can occur. We Americans are just not prepared for this possible eventuality.

Leon, when our son was only a young lad I recall I was starting to take some furniture up a steep stairway, and he said "Dad, do you think you should try to do that?" It was a strange feeling having one's child caution his own parent like that. Was it a harbinger of what would come some day? At the time it was something we sort of laughed about. The implications today are not so humorous.

We absorb the belief in our young, impressionable years that independence is a virtue. We expect adults to be able to look after themselves. Those who continue their dependence upon parents long after they have become adults are viewed with disfavor. Our whole culture, Leon, seems to be focused upon encouraging and maintaining the independence of citizens. Much of our condemnation of what we call welfare is probably based upon this fixation with independence. Adult citizens who we view as dependent upon the rest of us hard-working Americans, we look upon as failures.

Then, rather suddenly, in our brief experiences as a national culture, we have this increasing aging population on our hands.* We have made some efforts, as a nation, to assure some financial independence for the elderly, but little has really been done to prepare us psychologically to deal with the situation. For those of us caught up in it, to begin to become dependent more and more upon others, after years of experiencing our independence, is a rather traumatic experience.

In the last few years of my father's life I recall how he would frequently remark as we would help him in and out of places, "Isn't it terrible to be like this?" How he hated to be what he thought was a burden to his family.

Am I to experience a similar plight, Leon? I am just not prepared for it. I love my children dearly, but I don't want to surrender my independence to them or to anyone else. Are we older people players in what is culturally a national tragedy?

---

*At the present there is increasing concern over the aging of our population, and as debate on Social Security heats up, there is an underlying tone developing that aged citizens are really a drag and an undesirable restraint upon our nation's continued progress. Is this perspective really becoming more widespread, Leon?

The Simple Life

We originally planned to keep the place simple and easy to maintain, Leon. But as the years passed, these plans were eroded by supposed improvements. I am referring to our summer cabin. At the beginning we had no electricity and only a hand pump in the kitchen for drawing our water. Then electricity was added, soon to be followed by installing telephones. Later we modernized the building, including such "improvements" as two bathrooms, two furnaces, a water softener, water heater, sump pump, tempering tank, and television antenna. Now our place is indistinguishable from most modern urban residences.

I have made the remark to friends as they visit us and look at the equipment in our basement that one almost needs a degree in engineering to understand and maintain the conveniences that we have superimposed upon our original cabin. Leon, most of us have little, if any, knowledge of how this modern equipment operates and yet we keep purchasing more and more complicated machinery to control our homes! Can't we keep life about us more simple?

By our standards today, my grandmother lived a very simple life. She had few of the modern conveniences we believe necessary for a satisfying lifestyle. Yet I believe she was one of the more serene, contented, and well-adjusted individuals I have ever known. What does such a recollection tell me?

You know, we keep *padding* what we think is a decent standard of living. In fact, just what do we mean by a standard of living? Is there some absolute measurement by which we can gauge our level of living or is this an idea that reflects our increasing appetites for the new products that flood our market?* Where does it eventually end, Leon?

There is something about those few in our midst who live the more simple life that is attractive. For instance, they are not so dependent upon electronic equipment for their entertainment and consequently, when there is something like a power outage, they are not desperate in knowing what to do with their unsolicited spare time. Furthermore, they don't worry about having numerous reliable repair and maintenance people to keep the equipment in their homes in operation. They, themselves, can service most of the limited possessions they own.

More than refraining from loading their homes with all kinds of modern conveniences, these few people demonstrate simplicity in other ways as well. Often their view of the world about them is not cluttered with all the cynicism, skepticism, and sophistication many of us think necessary for a mature mind. They accept people as they are. Friendships are direct and trusted with few, if any, reservations. They find amusement, satisfaction, and rewards in many of the little daily occurrences in their environments. Observing a bird building its nest is as meaningful to them as attending a lecture by a famous scholar. They may regard the graceful strides of a deer in flight as being as marvelous and exciting as the operation of a new high speed, 200-plus MHz personal computer.

There are those who would consider these people naive in many respects, but there is something appealing about them for me, Leon. I wonder if they may not be in closer touch with the realities of our universe than many of us who think we are highly educated, sophisticated people.

There are some simple experiences that I never want to lose. Among these kinds of experiences are the following: the sense of awe over the varied beauties of nature; noticing the open, unadorned expression of inquisitiveness in a young child; awareness of the spontaneous look of affection from a loved one; receptiveness to your faithful pet dog looking at you in complete trust and confidence; enjoying the satisfaction that comes from creating and finishing some handmade artifact; realizing a certain kind of refreshment and relaxation that comes at the end of a task requiring considerable physical energy — you are tired but it feels good; consciousness of the gratification accompanying the non-verbal sharing of prized companionship with a dear friend; hearing the hearty laughter of another; perceiving the reassurance and confidence expressed by one in trouble when you appear; the willingness to pursue the excitement of promising rapport with new acquaintances; letting an experience register with you such as walking hand in hand down a tree-lined lane and realizing that your spouse by your side is your closest friend; stretching your emotional sensitivities to the place where your whole being quivers with a compassion for all of humanity.

Leon, help me to cherish such simplicities and ever expand upon them!

---

*Manufacturers and dealers are now investing much hope and resources in the belief that digital television will become considered as an absolute necessity in the standard of living for early twentieth-first century Americans. An advertising "blitz" will undoubtedly assure that this happens. The list keeps growing!

A "Centering" Place

Four decades ago when we purchased our lake property, hundreds of miles from our home then, I wondered about the wisdom of what we had done, Leon. We were renting our home and with our limited financial means we could not afford this newly acquired lakeshore and the down payment which would be required to buy a house where we were living. In a sense, were we "getting the cart before the horse" as the old saying goes?

But the benefits and rewards of what this beautiful, northern summer home would grow to mean to us were only dimly foreseen back then. We had spent many hours that summer searching the area for a place we liked which was not beyond our budget. We were very lucky, Leon, for we finally found an undeveloped plot of land in the midst of Minnesota lake country that was unsurpassed, as far as we were concerned, with the natural beauty it presented! We have been told that the Indian name for the sparkling lake we located on means "jewel of the north." Yes, Leon, we were indeed fortunate to find this place.

Our children grew up there in the summer. Now our grandchildren are following in their footsteps. Many memorable days were enjoyed with our parents and friends at our lake home. We struggled for many years trying to find a name for the place that was growing to mean so much for us. Finally, some summers ago the name "Francisco's Kum ba yah" burst upon us. Our place at last had a name!

Truly "Francisco's Kum ba yah" has been a gathering place. A place to share with family, friends, and individuals in many walks of life. A number of summers we even had ecumenical worship services each Sunday on our front lawn. The clear blue spring-fed waters of Ponto Lake provided the altar for these services. One visitor from Chicago once remarked that this was the most beautiful cathedral in which he had ever worshiped! Ah, the memories that are associated with our Kum ba yah, Leon!

Dietrich Bonhoeffer in his writings once referred to the retreat his family had in the Black Forest. He suggested that much of the fortitude and spiritual reserve he developed for those trying, fateful years in Nazi concentration camps may have been generated at their family gathering place. Who knows what similar kinds of inner strength may have been encouraged for many who have come to our place?

This has been a "centering" place for our family and friends, Leon. We have shared joys, ambitions, fears, and sorrows here. We have been able to lay aside the rush of outside activities and commune with nature, divinity, and the cosmos. We have been able to find direction in our lives. We have experienced the pulling together of family. We have found peace here at our "Kum ba yah."

As this is written on Thanksgiving Day, Leon, I have to give thanks for the opportunities our lake home has presented for meaningful growth in our lives. A wisdom beyond what little I may ever have had was at work four decades ago in guiding us to become stewards of this lake country property!

Struggling With Contemporary Life

"What e-mail has become for many is a high-tech illustration of a much broader paradox in this society: Our time seems to grow crowded in direct proportion to the technology we develop to uncrowd it." — Ralph Keyes

Leon, is there something about the evolution of civilization that "speeds up the clock"? Are there still a full twenty-four hours in each day?

Busy

"How have you been?"

"Busy!"

"What did you do over the weekend?"

"I kept busy!"

"How do you like retirement?"

"I'm busy as ever!"

What would we Americans do, Leon, if we did not have the word "busy" in our vocabulary to use? One wonders if this word is not the most overworked expression in our language? How true would the following description be of many of us?

Lord, we're a busy people.

We're too busy to hear the birds' songs.

We're too busy to see the flowers blooming.

We're too busy to observe the brilliant sunrise.

We're too busy to notice the glimmer in a child's eyes.

We're too busy to sense the wish of our children to play with us.

We're too busy to enjoy the companionship of our spouses.

We're too busy to have any sensitivity for the exhaustion of those close to us.

We're too busy to realize that our boss is really a human being.

We're too busy to discern the loneliness of our aging parents.

We're too busy to assist our needy neighbors.

We're too busy to correspond with friends.

We're too busy to read inspiring literature.

We're too busy to meditate.

We're too busy to hear your still, small voice, Lord.

We're too busy to die.

We're too busy to live.

What is happening to us, Leon?

Time-Weary Lives

More than I usually did with this part of the course, I was elaborating upon the concept of time and how culture affected our views of time. Then it occurred to me that there was an unusual kind of quietness in the classroom; suddenly it dawned upon me that these men were quite self-conscious about the concept of time. The members of this class were a group of prisoners at the Federal Penitentiary at Lewisburg, Pennsylvania! They were serving "time" and in this subculture, this subject had particular significance for them. I fear, Leon, until then, I was not as sensitive as I should have been to how various groups of people may be affected by their perspective of time.

We humans, especially here in the Western world, are driven by time, aren't we, Leon? We are a time-conscious people. We rush to keep appointments, to accomplish certain tasks by deadlines, to meet tight schedules. We are a time-weary people, are we not?

We tell others that we don't have time for a vacation, we don't have time to attend concerts, we don't have time to be with the family, we don't have time "to smell the roses"! We try to keep ahead of the many demands upon our lives and find some way we can squeeze out a few fleeting minutes of relaxation. But it is a real struggle to obtain even a few moments of real relaxation.

Do we ever stop to consider how our whole structure and arrangements of time are our own creations? There is nothing about this universe in which we live that reflects any intrinsic divisions of time such as we allow to govern our lives. We have written this script and then proceeded to become prisoners of it, haven't we?

Thomas Kelly has written how eternity surrounds us, pressing upon our time-torn lives.* During those rare moments when our minds break through the time-encrusted surroundings — the time barriers — in which our daily routine transpires, we catch glimpses of how futile it is to try to keep up with the kind of time we allow to govern our lives. We sense that we are wearing out our lives by artificially constructed time restraints.

The idea of eternity, when it does filter through to us, awakens us and sobers us. How truly inconsequential and unnecessary are many of our frantic efforts to master *the clock*! Our lives don't have to be the fragmented, harried, exhausted biographies that we make them. What does it take, Leon, for us to gain more of a steadying sense of eternity flowing through us and calming our frantic behavior? Whereas the Psalmist wrote long ago, "Be still and know that I am God," maybe we could add today, "Be still, repudiate the 'rat race' and know that I am God." Abandon the senseless, life-sapping treadmill and live! Be quiet. Listen. Fine-tune our full range of human sensitivities. Eternity envelops us.

---

*Kelly, Thomas R., *A Testament of Devotion* (Harper & Brother, 1941), p. 29.

Friendship Erosion

Soil erosion is a condition with which many of us are familiar, but another kind of erosion is not as frequently recognized, so it seems. I refer to friendship erosion. It is puzzling to me, Leon, how through the years many formerly dynamic, meaningful friendships erode. Friendships that were once significant, enjoyable, stimulating, supportive, creative, and prized fade into the background. A ritualistic exchange of greeting cards may occur during the holidays, but direct, personal contacts are no longer experienced. The years take their toll, don't they, on what were once vibrant, lively, cherished friendships?

Why does this happen, Leon? Perhaps one condition related to this occurrence is our mobility. Not until recent times have so many people been involved in frequent changes in their residences. Distance gradually extinguishes the warm fires of many friendships. For many of us when we move we know we are leaving behind friends that will never have the same meaning for us again. Well do I remember when we moved from Williamsport, Pennsylvania, many years ago. As we were driving out of our neighborhood, one elderly couple came out and stood in front of their house and with grim faces waved good-bye. Covert communication between us at that time signaled that the chances of us ever seeing one another again were not likely. And we never saw them again. One of the tragedies of modern life, Leon? I fear so!

There is another kind of mobility that enters the scene, too. These are changes that take place in our life positions. Variations and changes in education, interests, jobs, and lifestyles also are developments that contribute to another form of distance in friendships. We are reminded, for instance, of the many changes in employment that will and do occur in one's lifetime. Good friends we once worked with are abandoned all too often when we change jobs. In the expanding cosmopolitan world in which we live, steady, enduring friendships are difficult to maintain, aren't they?

Likely the factor of commitment is another consideration one should note, isn't it? To make and keep commitments to others, whether formally or informally understood, is lacking in many of our friendships. For many of us it seems that commitments to others imply restraints upon our freedom. Such commitments can interfere with other activities and interests. They can dampen our pursuit of varied pleasures. When old friends, for instance, phone from their distant homes and ask you to attend important anniversaries, the subject of your commitment to them becomes a pressing issue. Strong, enduring friendships require commitment, and in our busy lives this hampers our comforts and complicates our present schedules.

Furthermore, disciplined effort is likely another part of the picture of fading friendships. Keeping viable friendships does necessitate disciplined efforts to engage in such practices as picking up the phone occasionally to call others; it requires taking the time to sit down and write letters; it can compel us to plan and execute a trip to visit friends. Certainly effort is involved, e-mail notwithstanding! Friendship makes demands upon our time and plans. Few of us like to admit that we are lazy, but maybe, Leon, just plain laziness is present in our neglect of maintaining meaningful friendships. Slothful behavior does not support deep-rooted friendships. Retaining friendships often means subtracting time and effort from other activities in which we might wish to engage.

How important is the matter of priorities in this problem of eroding friendships? Maybe this is the root of the problem? Just what kind of value do we place upon our friendships? Are we disturbed by the need to examine our priorities from time to time and find out just how high or low a priority we give our friendships? Such inquiries are not encouraged in our society with its emphasis upon living for the pleasures of the moment.

What do we miss in this erosion of friendships, Leon? How much are our lives diminished because of this condition? Thinking about this subject makes me uneasy.

Focus On Behavior

When it comes to people that I know, I must confess that I have my likes and dislikes. I hope that those I like outnumber those whom I dislike, but there definitely are individuals I have known whom I dislike. For instance, egotistical, swaggering, macho, overbearing individuals definitely turn me off. I fear I would like to tell them in some forceful manner what disgusting, offensive, repelling individuals they are. Similarly, sarcastic, pretentious, omniscient, clever-appearing individuals produce negative reactions in me. For individuals who possess these characteristics, I erect social distances that block meaningful communication with them. I fear I find very little that is lovable about such individuals. I wish I did not possess these feelings, Leon, but I do.

These individuals are especially subject to unfavorable judgments on my part. It is all I can do at times to avoid actually hating some of these people. And yet at the same time, I am partly aware of the adverse effect this is having on me. In such situations I am forgetting my ideal of attempting to see something of the spark of divinity in all humans. I also shut out any efforts to engage in dialogue with them. Ideals are diluted that I would like to follow more consistently. In many ways my dislike for these individuals penalizes and injures me. I bring much of my discomfort on myself.

I have worked on this problem, Leon, but I have not done too well with it. Many years ago I realized, at least theoretically, that I could foster a much better attitude toward myself and initiate better relationships with others if I could separate individuals' behavior and actions from the person himself/herself. I well remember going to some faculty meetings where I would endeavor to remind myself of this need to make this kind of separation. Then before I knew it some obnoxious faculty member would get up to speak and I would think to myself what a "big bag of air" this individual was. Consistently, to distinguish the person from his or her behavior is a very difficult assignment to practice.

Failure to succeed, at least partially, in this kind of distinction can contaminate human relationships — even with those whom you have loved. In the marriage and family classes I used to emphasize the difference between what is referred to as constructive quarreling and destructive quarreling between husband and wife. In constructive quarreling, the focus is upon the behavior of the other. For instance, "I don't think you should have spent so much money on that new lawn chair." The attention here is pointed toward excessive spending behavior. In destructive quarreling the focus is upon the other person himself or herself. Here one might say to the other, "You don't have any sense at all about spending money." This kind of attack in quarreling cuts to the core of the other's personality. One's ego is wounded and frequent encounters of this kind can and do send many marriages to the divorce courts.

Why can't we refrain from harshly judging the personalities of others? Whether it be individuals we assume we don't like or people close to us when we judge something about them, why can't we focus on their behavior, Leon? When others say or do something we dislike, are we unable to avoid slipping into the habit of tearing down their very selves by our careless judgments? How differently we might get along with others if we more often made this distinction between the behavior and the very core personality of people.

Writers like Joan Borysenko stress the importance of doing this for one's mental and spiritual health. In a passage on the meaning of forgiveness that touches on this matter, she writes, "Forgiveness means accepting the core of every human being as the same as yourself and giving them the gift of not judging them."* She proceeds to point out that we may criticize others' behavior, but we should attempt to check our criticism of the person himself/herself. In a way, this seems like a subtle, perhaps insignificant drawing of lines, but I believe it has tremendous implications for ourselves and how we get along with others.

Leon, why is this such a difficult assignment to put into action? Are most of us such insecure, immature, unsteady individuals that we think we derive some kind of propping up by downgrading and judging others? Is it because we are careless in how we engage in our relationships with others? Is it because we are mentally lazy and don't want to make the effort to make this distinction between the actual person and his or her behavior?   I don't really know why this is such a difficult assignment, but I do know it is for me.

---

*Borysenko, Joan, *Minding the Body, Mending the Mind* (New York: Bantam Books, 1988), p. 176.

Sucker!

Not often, Leon, do I recall overtly referring to other people as gullible individuals, but I know I have thought this about them. It is not considered a compliment to be called gullible. None of us likes to be thought of as naive, shallow, easily deceived personalities. We are insulted when we are called "suckers"! But in all truth, Leon, don't all of us Americans live in a highly orchestrated, deception-producing culture? Is it not almost impossible to avoid often being "suckers"?

Are we not led by our advertising world, for instance, to believe that if we only buy the beauty products, the household items, the new automobiles, the latest sports equipment, the fastest computers, and so forth that the good life will be ours? Are we not increasingly exposed to clever appeals by lotteries, casinos, and other games of chance to believe that only if we win big will we have achieved the ultimate in life? Is not the American Dream, Leon, equated with possessing "the goodies" with which the advertising world deluges us? Contentment, comfort, tranquillity, and fulfillment follow, supposedly, do they not, with the acquisition of this American Dream? Gullible? Fooled? Deceived?

Such uncritical thinking and living ignores the wisdom emphasized in the writings and thought of the great teachers of the past and present, doesn't it? Have not these perceptive minds in various ways exposed the foolishness of believing that enduring happiness is something we can acquire by the acquisition of the perishable merchandise flashed before us by the advertising industry? Can we not learn how insatiable our appetites can become by succumbing to the "lures" of those who gain by our gullibility? Can we avoid the intoxication which so often overtakes us as we unwittingly buy into this perverted American Dream?

There do seem to be individuals, Leon, who escape from being suckers, from becoming slavish creatures of our consumer culture, from becoming trapped people unable to realize the futility of the popularized American Dream. Such individuals live quite modestly. They manage to live without automobiles, television sets, air conditioning, dishwashers, riding lawn mowers, and so forth. They avoid being burdened with conveniences that frequently need repair or replacement. They have simple tastes. Their lives reflect an inner kind of depth and harmony that makes us uneasy. They disturb us with what some would say are their counterculture tendencies. They challenge our priorities. They make us wonder if there is really much of lasting value in all the possessions we think necessary to have for our contentment. Whether we fully realize it or not, they unmask the deceptive nature of much of contemporary living.

Leon, I have been a good, steady consumer of much of what is "peddled" before us in the commercial world. My appetite to buy, buy, buy has shown few signs of abating. Yet I have long been uncomfortably aware that the acquisition of these material objects brings only fleeting satisfaction. I have allowed the culture which surrounds me to confuse my priorities. I, like most of those around me, have been a gullible individual. I need guidance, Leon, in more steadfastly pursuing those goals and objectives in life which are not compromised by the hypnotizing din of our advertising world. Daily, I need direction in my life if worthy priorities are to be retained.

Disillusionment

Would it not be a much better world in which to live if the world actually was more like we picture it in childhood? Ashley Montagu has written a book, *Growing Young,* in which he says the problem of children is that they grow up! We find as we grow up that the world is not nearly the kind of world we pictured it to be when we were children. Adults complicate the world, especially the environment in which they dwell with other humans. There is not the honesty, forthrightness, spontaneity, trust, and so forth among adults that there is among children, is there, Leon?

Early in adulthood many of us begin to find out that people operate on a plane considerably different from that which our young, naive minds used to think was the case. We begin to experience disillusionment, and our heroes, promises, and ideals begin to crumble. It is difficult to have our eyes opened to the realities of the adult world.

One of my early disillusionments was when I was an undergraduate. I was on a student committee to help select an inspiring speaker to address a student-faculty audience. In order to stir the minds of students, we had been told that we wanted to secure the most outstanding, inspiring public speaker that we could bring to the campus. But soon in the committee meeting, the conversation directed by the faculty advisers, began to concentrate on what individual would be most politically advantageous to the university if we would invite him or her as our speaker. The idea of an *inspiring* speaker was soon discarded in deference to whom we could invite who would strengthen his or her support for the needs of the university. So much for inspiration for the students. It was a disillusioning experience, Leon.

Another type of disillusionment that I have never made my peace with concerns the rationality and civility of university faculties. When I first became part of a college faculty, I thought I would be among brilliant men and women who would definitely conduct their business in a rational manner. Joining the ranks of highly educated people, I thought, would place me among individuals who had abandoned petty, jealous, self-seeking behavior, and I also thought that intellectual pursuits and the championing of scholarly ideas and goals would prevail among such esteemed teachers. Was I ever in for a letdown, Leon! The intrigue, the petty dealings, the deceptions, the irrational accusations, and so forth seemed especially to prosper on college campuses. (I almost thought the dominant course in graduate school that many faculty members had taken had been in A. P. 450 — Advanced Pettiness 450!) Not uncommon was the condition where faculty members would not speak to one another because of some earlier conflict they had experienced. Life among educated college faculty was no different from the rest of the adult world, Leon. Apparently there is no association between the amount of education individuals achieve and their ability to be civil. It is a disillusioning experience and I have never made my peace with this reality of campus life!

Yet do we humans have to eliminate idealism in our thinking and hopes for human relationships? Cannot we foster good will among people, wherever we may be, even though we may often encounter rejection of our efforts? If we just succumb to this adult world of lies, dishonesty, pettiness, meanness, and so forth, where does this leave us?

Maybe we should look upon the task of some of us to be that leaven in the social body that can promise in time to lift the plane of our interactions with one another. Is such a view too childlike, Leon? If so, is this kind of childlike view maybe something that is sorely needed in our hardened adult world? Cannot wisdom perhaps temper some of our childish views, but preserve the core of childlike trust, honesty, and integrity?

Bureaucratic Prisons

Writers such as Kenneth Boulding have stated that the real revolution of modern times is the *organizational revolution*. Throughout the industrialized world, governmental, industrial/business, educational, and religious organizations more and more dominate our lives. The impersonal bureaucratic form these organizations take is so much a part of our social landscape, Leon, that I fear we often fail to comprehend how extensively our lives are controlled by them. For one who really craves freedom of thought and action, might one's plea for help be phrased somewhat as follows?

"I want to be free; I want to think original thoughts unencumbered by any censorship from superior authorities.

"I want to be able to probe myself and develop whatever creative abilities I may possess without fear of being deprived of making some kind of a respectable living.

"I want choices for a realistic livelihood not to be limited to just spirit-crushing openings in some indifferent work organization.

"If need be, I want to be different without being scorned by those with whom I associate.

"In some ways I guess I want to be a 'loner,' where I can be comfortable in my isolation.

"But yet, I also want to be able to be a meaningful part of larger groupings where what I do and what I say does count for something.

"Being some kind of automaton frightens me.

"I don't want to end up being a cog in some giant human machine.

74

"Can I avoid being entrapped by today's power centers?

"Can I be true to myself, to my aspirations, to whatever wellsprings of creativity I possess and still be a vitally functioning member of the world in which I live?

"I want to be free. I want to be free."

Is this freedom urge a vain hope in modern life, Leon? Is it a kind of delusion that our leaders foist upon us? One wonders.

Meanness

New owners acquire a private social service facility.

An agreement accompanies this acquisition that the present staff will be retained.

Then services of the director are terminated.

And so it goes, Leon.

Are our social organizations — charitable organizations, business organizations, educational organizations, religious organizations — riddled by mean people?

Do petty jealousy, power hunger, recognition cravings dominate the lives of "organizational people"?

Does the typical bureaucratic organization that engulfs the lives of most of us foster the "mean game" in us, Leon?

Are directors, supervisors, department heads, and so forth constantly in danger of being subverted by covetous "underlings"?

Are "peer workers" in an unending struggle to outmaneuver one another for promotions?

Are our organizations crowded by individuals who will stop at nothing to obtain the positions, the rewards, the recognition they want?

Is endless litigation by malcontents ever to cease stifling organizational creativity?

In our organizational life, where is good will today, Leon?

As individuals enter into and function in their various organizations, where is that divine spark, that inner light that I still believe we human creatures possess?

Leon, the life of a hermit *does have* its appeal!

"Pin-Pricking"

A serious discussion was under way in one of the university's key administrative-faculty committees. The topic centered around whether or not to initiate a closed stack policy in regard to checking out books from the university library. Members were deploring the fact that so many books were being lost by students taking them without processing them with the desk check-out. As a young faculty member, I interrupted the flow of the discussion by saying I had just read where a prominent Columbia University professor had written that a school should feel complimented when students were running away with library books! Often library books were not that popular with students! There was a pause in the deliberations of the committee and the academic dean said, "You would expect Francisco to say that!"

Leon, my sociological education early instilled within me a *debunking motif.* I have never been able to conclude whether this has been a curse or a blessing! I must confess that there have been times that inwardly I have enjoyed engaging in this kind of behavior. There is something about being in the presence of self-important, pompous, grim individuals that appears almost automatically to trigger this debunking tendency. A price has been paid for this kind of behavior, I fear, in that it does not contribute to one's being a popular person in many groups.

Does debunking play a needed role in our lives and in the life of our society? Is there, for instance, a place for "sobering up" Congressional members who in their ambitious zeal make exaggerated claims about how they are going to revolutionize the country? Is there a justifiable reason for endeavoring to awaken individuals to greater sanity when they are carried away with unrealistic, unfounded, questionable beliefs and activities?

Is there a connection between the debunking role and the prophetic role? I wonder if there is not a relationship with more responsible debunking and prophetic insights? Of course there is a kind of debunking that carelessly belittles the claims and assumptions of individuals without any valid basis for doing so. Here a destructive behavior can capture one where one enjoys just upsetting individuals for no reason at all. But constructive, perceptive debunking would seem to play an important role in helping us humans from being carried away in unwise and harmful pursuits, would it not, Leon?

I fear that this debunking motif is almost second nature with me in many instances. Having been trained to note and perceive long-term implications of many social policies, I cannot help myself when I note the foolishness of many leaders' appeals.* Debunking, I believe, can be a means of exposing many kinds of fallacies and short-sightedness. Such, though, does need to be tempered with compassion and understanding, does it not, Leon? Care has to be exercised that debunking what others believe does not seriously endanger the core of their self-image. In other words, I guess one must recognize that debunking can be a dangerous tool. Help me to strive to use this training I have had in a constructive and responsible manner.

---

*Occasionally I write a letter to the editor. Not long ago I wrote a letter to the local newspaper editor on a subject that was stirring considerable debate. In the letter I combined a debunking perspective along with some cynicism. I asked Barbara to read what I had written and when I asked her what she thought of it, she replied, "It is fine what you have written here, but no one will know what you are talking about!" Maybe I should have resigned then and there from any further use of debunking as a tool of social criticism.

Could We?

If we were in a tour group visiting the Grand Canyon and one of the members of the group kept asking the guide questions about what kind of an endowment does Harvard University have and what is really the favorite sports event for Americans, we would think such a person was, what we might say, completely "out-of-line" with such questions. This person never asked about how the Grand Canyon might have been formed, when it was discovered, what kind of geological formations dominate the walls of the canyon, and so forth. This person did not have any questions to ask the guide that were related to the Grand Canyon. Obviously he was missing the opportunity to obtain greater knowledge of this famous natural wonder.

Yet, Leon, may not many of us be engaged in similar behavior and not realize it? Is it not very likely that we are asking trivial and irrelevant questions about the universe? Some writers referring to scientific exploration have said one of the problems of science may be that humans are asking the wrong questions about the universe. Are we missing the mark when it comes to asking the really important and relevant questions about the universe of which we are a part? Could it be that our descendants many generations down the line will look back on us and wonder how we could have been so far off-base in the kind of questions we were asking?

Similarly, how many of us are capable of asking and prepared to ask the really important questions about our lives? Do we not waste much time and energy pursuing goals and activities that belittle our lives simply because we have not stopped to try and ask really important questions about ourselves? Do we dare to inquire about what we could be doing to develop more fully our unique personalities? Is a kind of courage and effort required to ask such questions?

What would most of us do, Leon, if we found ourselves in a situation where we were in the presence of an unusually wise person who had great powers of insight into the lives of individuals and this seer gave us the opportunity to ask five important questions about our lives that she would endeavor to answer for us? Would not most of us be very uncomfortable and ill-prepared to profit from such an experience?

Leon, what would be among the five most important and relevant questions I might ask about my life? Would you pass or fail me on the questions I might create and ask?

Missing The Mark

We were visiting with my 94-year-old uncle. Usually our conversations were about such subjects as the weather, gardening, fishing, traveling, and so on. So often with individuals, particularly with elderly people, we fail to touch on matters of deep concern to them. The struggles, pain, confining life, and health concerns of elderly individuals we can too easily gloss over and pitch our conversations on a rather superficial plane. So, I thought, I shall open the door for conversing on another level of discourse.

Consequently, I said, "If I had a magic wand or power to provide our lives with the drive, vigor, and abilities that we had forty or fifty years ago, I would be tempted to do so. I could take some of that. Couldn't you?" And to my surprise, my uncle replied, "No. I wouldn't want that. I wouldn't want to have to go through many of the things I did back then. I told my family recently that what I would like to have for Christmas would be a Cadillac with a chauffeur!"

Leon, how often do we miss the mark when we are wanting to talk with others about more serious subjects? I fear we misunderstand and misjudge others more frequently than we realize. Especially with elderly people, I wonder how well we really understand them. In spite of all the research and writing that has been done the last few decades in the field of gerontology, how well do we really know and understand specific elderly people? Don't we tend to project upon older people some of the conclusions from these writings that may or may not apply to particular older individuals?

One is repelled with the sight of a worker in an institution for the elderly talking to the residents as if they were three-year-olds, but to shift conversation to greater-in-depth exchange of thought may involve more knowledge of the particular individual we endeavor to talk with than we had expected. Even in my family, I had this experience.

Leon, isn't this a part of a larger problem for us humans? Don't we too often fail to try to understand individuals as individuals? Don't we too often categorize and classify them by their age, by their group affiliations and other stereotypes, and miss the chance to carry on significant conversation with them? Even with us professionals who have had formal training in understanding human behavior, may we not even more grievously err in our understanding of specific individuals with whom we work? Isn't there the danger of deluding ourselves that the knowledge we possess automatically provides us with *accurate* insights into others?

Leon, let the experience with my 94-year-old uncle make me cautious in approaching other individuals with efforts to initiate serious conversation with them. May such experiences, however, not be used as excuses to fail to make efforts to tune in to them and when opportunities arise, listen to their deeper thoughts and concerns. And may I ever be receptive to learning from them, regardless of their age!

Unprepared

I just have to recognize the fact, Leon, that I am not prepared for any great fame or acclaim. If I had ever achieved widespread recognition and been highly successful in some endeavor, I fear I would have been a typical, egotistical, overbearing celebrity! I might have feigned humility, but inside, I would have possessed an ego of inflated dimensions.

This awareness, however, has had another effect upon me. I have, I believe, been more fearful of success than failure. Projects that have appeared to be developing into quite successful undertakings, bringing distinction to me for the key leadership roles I played, I have backed away from. I did not want to be placed in a position where I could really have to find out if I could handle such success. In most cases, Leon, I just don't like to be in the limelight!

It's not that I don't have an annoying ego. Like most of us humans, I have a craving for recognition and praise. Furthermore, I have experienced my share of times in which I secretly envied the success of others. I have had my daydreams of becoming a renowned scholar, writer, or speaker. But then when I have more soberly projected myself into circumstances where some kind of unusual acclaim might be bestowed upon me, I retreat. Is this really a form of cowardice on my part, Leon? Or is there more than this involved in this behavior of mine?

Our American society is a culture that certainly gives much attention to our celebrities in movies, athletics, politics, business, and so on. We are told as youngsters that individuals in America can, if they strive enough, experience a log cabin to the White House, a rags to riches, a plodding actor to a famous theatrical star, a play lot baseball player to a big leaguer, kind of career. We read and hear over and over again the success stories of famous Americans. The urge to be successful is in the air we breathe, Leon.

Yet how many of us have any idea of the price that such success may demand of us? Do we realize what this may do to our relationships with others? Do we have any idea of how we as individuals may be affected? Do we sense how this old-fashioned thing called "character" may be greatly altered by our drives to succeed?

When I stop to think about it, Leon, I just know that I am not prepared for the kind of fame and limelight that this American success version would bring to me. Yet through most of my life I have wished to provide meaningful and constructive leadership in groups of which I am a part. Leon, some of us Americans can find ourselves in a frustrating situation here. It is possible, isn't it, to accomplish some worthwhile tasks for yourself and others without having to shoulder the task of being successful with your success?

How About Humor?

When the Japanese were bombing Pearl Harbor, the story is told that when American soldiers were running out of one of the barracks, one of them suddenly started to turn back in order to secure his false teeth which he had forgotten. His buddy yelled to him, "Come on. Those Japs aren't dropping lollipops!"

Whether or not this story is actually true, it does remind us of the important function of humor in critical moments. So often when we are in the midst of very serious experiences, we forget how humor can reduce the gravity of the situation and enable us to clear our heads for more reasonable thought and action. Leon, help me never to lose a sense of humor.

Back in the turbulent sixties, some of the scholars writing about the leaders of the counterculture cautioned about those leaders who showed no sense of humor. One writer, Peter Berger, warned about zealous, passionate leaders and recommended that individuals watch for leaders' ability to laugh. Is there not considerable truth in this, Leon? Is not the absence of genuine humor in a leader a good indication that such a person is so rigidly wrapped up with oneself that he or she cannot perceive some levity in one's thought or behavior? Lack of humor, may it not reflect intoxication with oneself?

Likely, we overlook the fact that some of the greatest leaders, even spiritual leaders like Jesus, possessed more humor than is generally recognized. Elton Trueblood once wrote a book on the humor of Christ. Most likely Jesus did perceive much humor in the lives and events that surrounded him. His parables reflect what is probably a rich humor concerning the worries, follies, and troubles of humans. When we read about Jesus saying to religious leaders of his time, "Alas for you, blind guides! You say, 'If a man swears by the sanctuary, that is nothing; but if he swears by the gold in the sanctuary, he is bound by his oath' "* — there is not only scorn being shown here, but most likely a humorous insight as well. Do we, Leon, perhaps ignore the humor present in the lives and thought of some of our greatest spiritual leaders?

Sooner or later all of us will experience trying moments in our lives. We may fear losing our jobs, worry about our marriages dissolving, feel threatened by health problems, fret with the prospects of severe economic reversals, and so forth. Such grave periods in one form or another are bound to enter our lives. If we are able to introduce some humor into these anxieties, can we not, Leon, often manage to break these paralyzing spells? Does not humor possess the saving potential of so lightening the burdens of such periods in our lives that new insights can occur whereby solutions emerge for resolving our difficulties?

Recently, I was facing surgery. I was experiencing considerable anxiety about it. Then my oldest daughter, who is a registered nurse, gave me a completely exaggerated account of the surgery to an extent that was ridiculous, and I saw the humor which she was communicating. The overdrawn, momentous nature of the prospects of what was facing me was reduced and I could view the matter through calmer eyes. Thank you, Leon, I would say, for the presence of humor in our lives. May I never stifle this necessary factor for sane living.

---

*Matthew 23:16 NEB

Some Guideline Questions

Unbridled, unrestrained, blind ethnocentrism frightens me, Leon. It is almost unbelievable what some individuals, intoxicated with the tribalism of their religious fanaticism, ethnic loyalties, or national zeal will do to those who are considered their enemies. Recent events in the Balkans, Northern Ireland, and the Near East are among the examples of such extreme ethnocentrism to scourge humanity in the closing decades of this supposedly civilized century. If such unchecked ethnocentrism cannot soon be transformed to global benefits by our human race, I fear the future for our species is precarious, to say the least.

But the belief that there are no values or ethics that are universally applicable is almost as disturbing to me, Leon. Among some scholarly groups a kind of relativism has been accepted that dismisses any attempts to seek and understand standards of conduct and policy making that have some universal validity. This thinking has even been extended to the assertion that everything in human thought and belief is relative to the individual. Simply stated, there are those who claim that the only way of judging what is true, what is beautiful, what is good, is what is held as such for a particular individual. This leaves us humans prisoners of our own subjectivism, does it not? How can we then communicate meaningful, intelligent, understandable points of view to others? Such scholarship, I suspect, largely ignores the epistemological ramifications of such extreme relativism. Again the net effects of such an outlook can easily be that "anything goes." One has no way of judging or evaluating the thought and behavior of others.

For those who take the problems of contemporary humanity seriously though, there are some real difficulties in finding avenues of thought and action that avoid both the dangers of ethnocentrism and relativism. On our shrinking planet how are we to direct our thinking and behavior as we come in contact more and more with "strange bedfellows"? Who is right? Who is wrong? No wonder, is there, that many people today are confused and upset with all the conflicting voices that claim their religion, their national views, their belief system is the true one?

Broadening influences such as education, travel, and cross-cultural contacts can rather easily leave many individuals in a quandary. As old "security posts" of belief are shaken by such experiences, what can one believe today? This dilemma continues to trouble me, Leon. I don't believe there is any easy answer for resolving this philosophical, sociological, anthropological difficulty. Nevertheless, some kind of effort needs to be attempted to begin to resolve this intellectual problem that has all too many real results for the fate of humankind.

When situations arise, then, in which one is confronted with conflicting views of what is true, what is beautiful, what is good, these guideline questions would seem to be helpful. These questions I base upon the lectures of some of my most influential teachers at Drake and Duke Universities and upon reading I have done related to the subject.

How do views in question affect the unity of humans? Do they tend to divide or unify humans? Do the views tend to reach out and be more inclusive of others or are they exclusive in how they affect others?

Do the views attempt to take into consideration the accumulated knowledge of serious, dedicated thinkers from a wide range of different cultures or are they confined to the limited perspectives of individuals in only one or a few cultures?

Do the views possess creative potential for widening the scope of one's understanding of the cosmos or do they bind one into a stagnant mold?

Do the views reflect a respect for the dignity of human individuals or do they demean in obvious or subtle ways the human individual?

Do the views indicate an awareness of the integrated, sensitive ties of humans with other living creatures and with the ecosystem?

Do the views encourage the emancipation of the human spirit and intellect from conditions which may have been checking human creativity or upon close inspection do they suggest manipulation by "power-seekers"? How do the views impact upon vested interests?

Do the views recognize that human knowledge and understanding is ever-expanding, changing, and being revised? In this respect, do the views appear to have more of an underlying "ring" of humility or arrogance?

Granted, these questions are not, by any means, a comprehensive formulation of the guidelines which can be applied to beginning to resolve the dangers of ethnocentrism or cultural relativism, but could these not be a starting point? I would hope, Leon, that my own thinking can be refined and new insights can be gained on this subject.

Spiritual Restlessness

"Simply by doing its cognitive job, sociology puts the institutional order and its legitimating thought patterns under critical scrutiny."
— Peter L. Berger

Leon, can one study intensely in a discipline like sociology and not develop a certain restlessness with contemporary institutional life?

Sabbath Made For Man

A conscientious young couple is trying to provide janitorial services for their church, and they are severely reprimanded by the minister for not clearing with him every change they make in the appearance of the building.* A creative student is marked low by her professor for failing to follow minutely all the directions that the instructor had given for writing original essays. A customer is ignored by the store personnel because he appears to be too boorish to be shopping in their exclusive shop. A client is denied benefits by a government agency because she failed to answer one question on the form she was supposed to fill out.

What is happening in these examples of human beings receiving ill-considered treatment by such people? What do parishioners, students, customers, and clients such as these have in common? Does it suggest that all is not well with our institutions? I believe it does, Leon.

Long is the history of human institutions thwarting the fulfillment of human needs. Leaders in these institutions lose sight of the original goals and purposes of religious, educational, business, and government institutions. They seem to forget, Leon, that these human efforts came into existence to meet certain basic human needs such as helping fulfill the quest of humans for spiritual understanding or to aid individuals in their efforts to secure certain commodities to make their lives more pleasant. Leaders in institutions all too often it seems come to think these institutions exist exclusively for them. In various ways they indicate that parishioners, students, customers, and clients obstruct the smooth operation of their institutions. Churches come to function, too frequently it seems, for the benefit of the clergy and church officials; schools revolve around meeting the satisfactions of the faculty and administrators; businesses become the exclusive domain of the managers; and branches of government come to exist for the satisfaction and security of the elected and appointed officials.

It is no wonder, Leon, that there is widespread discontent and frustration in our world, is there? Increasingly there are those who bemoan how citizens are losing faith in their institutions and yet seem to be oblivious to what may be involved here. Don't they sense that the human creations that people are so dependent upon for the satisfaction of basic needs all too often inhibit the meeting of these needs? Too often individuals who may want greater spiritual fulfillment have to obtain such in spite of the religious organizations that exist supposedly to help nourish the satisfaction of this need; too often individuals who want to achieve an education have to do so in spite of our schools; too often individuals who endeavor to have their most basic survival needs gratified cannot depend upon available businesses to meet such needs; too often eligible individuals who need certain government services have to endure all kinds of complications and personal indignities by branches of government in receiving these services. It is almost a maddening world at times, it seems.

This problem was recognized long ago, wasn't it? When Jesus was reminding people in his time that the Sabbath was made for man and not man for the Sabbath, was he not saying our institutions come into existence to meet the needs of us humans, not to use us humans as impersonal instruments to grind up in the complexities of institutional life? Leon, why has this truth seemed to evade so long and so often the leadership of our institutions?

What would happen if our institutions would really begin to function on a wide scale so that real, consistent, continued efforts would be made to see that these institutions were actually responding to the contemporary needs of the individuals they originally developed to serve? What would life be like if when we attended our churches, synagogues, and so forth, we knew we would find spiritual fulfillment? What would happen to us if we knew we could definitely obtain meaningful, significant education in our schools? What would be the effect upon customers if they knew when they went to business organizations to satisfy basic economic wants that they could be assured that their best interests were really important to the owners and managers of these businesses? What if branches of government could always be counted on to give serious priority to meeting the needs of individual citizens and clients? Are such questions reflecting entirely utopian thought, Leon? I hope not.

----

*This actually happened in a church with which the author is acquainted.

Frustrated Spiritual Hunger

While I know that it was an erroneous impression, when I used to travel on the old highways through the mountains of western North Carolina and eastern Tennessee and in the morning observe the residents of cabins sitting in their rocking chairs, I thought these people didn't seem to have a care in the world. Here I was in graduate study at Duke University and struggling to understand complex social issues, involved theological and ethical questions, and puzzling circumstances of human existence, while these people in a seemingly innocent manner enjoyed a life free from any worry about these many subjects that disturbed me. I tended to envy them.

In a somewhat similar manner today, I envy many church people who seem to adjust easily to their church life and show no signs of being bothered by numerous conditions which I see existing in our churches. I would like very much to find a church home in which I could consistently enter into worship services that were inspiring, partake with no reservations in the social activities of the parish, and contribute generously to the work of the church without doubting that my contributions were going for really worthy and significant causes. But some rebellious, questioning, disquieting force within me seems to prevent me from enjoying this kind of identity and association with a church. For many years I have experienced this frustration, and the struggle, I fear, has not improved with age, Leon.

I believe that we humans are religious individuals. We yearn to feel a vital connection with something larger and more significant than ourselves. Organized religion, I used to think, was a vehicle for making possible such a linkage. But more often than not, it seems to stand in the way. I remember a number of years ago a retired clergyman saying that all too often when he went to church, so disappointed and disillusioned was he with the services that he came out feeling more like cursing under his breath than being inspired to praise God. Leon, I fear that like other institutionalized areas of life, such as schools, which instead of facilitating learning actually often inhibit it, organized religion frustrates the search for God rather than enhances it. If we shed our innocence, is this the price we have to pay?

What are some of my complaints, Leon? They are many. Here are a few of them. All too frequently the subject of the clergyman's message may not be relevant to my present concerns and thoughts. What he or she says is meaningless to me. I just can't command myself to fit the particular worship theme chosen by others.

Although this may be changing in a number of churches, often there is little spontaneity in the worship service. The order of worship, the hymns, the music, the scriptures, the responses, and so forth are planned ahead of time and may or may not mesh with the mood of those actually present for a given worship service. If one thinks about what is happening, a sense of estrangement and distance between the pulpit and the congregation too often exists.

In this setting, the formal ritual followed is more or less mechanically observed. No explicit explanation is given why these particular parts of the worship and ritual are being chosen and utilized. No link between the present circumstances of people with long-observed rituals is given and too often the clergyman shows a failure to project his or her own feelings into the ritual, with the result being a monotone-like presentation. Little progress seems to have been made with many worship leaders from early grade school when as children they got up in public and dully recited the pieces that had been given them by their teachers.

The often ancient symbolism utilized in worship services, while bearing a rich heritage, is not made meaningful to the present circumstances in which many of us find ourselves. Religious artifacts, robes, creeds, and so on are supposed to remind us of profound, moving experiences of past peoples and leaders. Too often today, I fear, they are at most just aesthetically pleasing to many people. They fail in helping us to relate our own lives to the underlying issues of human existence.

These are a few of the complaints about many of our worship services, Leon. I sometimes wonder if our worship leaders are just mentally lazy and don't want to make the effort to explain how what they are saying, the symbolism that surrounds them, and the tools of worship observed in a given service can provide needed answers and sustenance for contemporary living.

I hunger, Leon, for spiritual food, but it is a rare experience when I receive much spiritual nourishment in the services of organized religion. I really do not wish to regress to the naiveté of my childhood days in order to try to remedy this situation, but neither do I glory in the discontents of my adulthood.

Out Of Control?

What would our world be like, Leon, if every human experienced during his lifetime a profoundly moving, mystical, spiritual experience? In a Sociology of Religion class I had related what to me was a deeply stirring television movie. It was a true account about the young son of a famous World War II reporter/writer who bravely and gallantly struggled with a terminal illness. The movie ended with his eventual death and a sense that one had observed drama so deeply shaking that words were completely inadequate in describing what one had witnessed.

A man in the class responded by saying he, too, had seen the movie and he was more or less bored by it. I was unprepared for this response, Leon. I had been unable to comprehend how anyone could watch this presentation and not be deeply affected by it. A truth was driven home to me though. Not every human being apparently experiences soul-stirring times and events. I wonder and suspect that there are individuals who go through life unaware of the "subterranean currents" of human existence that play upon us.

Are those scholars correct who assert that religion is really an art and not all humans cultivate this potential in their lives? Does every human even have this potential? Whatever the actuality may be here, I am troubled, Leon, that there are fellow humans who never get to the "mountaintops" in their lifetime. If so, are they deprived of that which invests our existence with what may be our most distinctive characteristic — that which most differentiates us from other known forms of life?

Are not our religious institutions formed to nourish, direct, and refine "that" which may be our most distinctive characteristic as humans? But do they accomplish this with appreciable numbers of their adherents? Would many of their leaders really want individuals in their congregations and parishes who had been to the "mountaintop"? Would such leaders feel threatened by the presence of these individuals? I don't know, Leon, but I am suspicious here.

A major purpose of our institutions is to control our behavior, and the presence of large numbers of people who have experienced deeply moving religious experiences might create situations where conditions could easily get out of hand.* We wouldn't dare to want this to happen, would we, Leon? Or would we?

———————————

*After all, look what happened to the parent Jewish religious institution when Jesus' disciples, filled with the religious experiences they had had, were "turned loose" in their culture!

Until —

As long as there is one hungry person, Leon, I will not be comfortable when I eat.

As long as there is one inadequately clad human, Leon, I will be uneasy when I look in my closet full of clothes.

As long as there is one emaciated child, Leon, I will be aware of the contrast with my healthy grandchildren.

As long as there is one homeless wanderer, Leon, I will be embarrassed with the luxuries of my home.

As long as there are beggars on our streets, Leon, I will find enjoyment in random shopping dampened.

As long as there are diminishing supplies of fuel, Leon, I will be self-conscious when I consume these fuels for pleasure rides.

As long as individuals are deprived of the basic essentials for living, Leon, I will find no satisfaction in pursuing the acquisition of expensive items.

As long as there is one being unnecessarily suffering, Leon, I will not boast of my wellness.

As long as hatred and violence are encouraged, Leon, I will not experience peace.

As long as manipulative politicians focus attention upon the poor as scapegoats for complex social problems, Leon, I cannot be optimistic about the future of our country.

As long as vain people abuse power, I cannot be indifferent to the plight of the powerless.

As long as there are individuals who take advantage of defenseless others, I shall continue to engage in what some would dub futile breast-beating.

As long as I inhabit this earth, Leon, I cannot sense the quietude I seek while there is discord anywhere.

"... But For The Grace Of God"

"Don't criticize another until you have walked a mile in his moccasins" is attributed to an old Indian proverb, isn't it, Leon? Are there limitations to the application of this? Aren't there individuals who are so despicable that we can't even come close to imagining ourselves in their moccasins?

Leon, I have frequently thought that "there but for the grace of God go I" about a wide variety of individuals whose behavior and lives are repugnant to me. Yet, with effort, I have also recognized that they are human beings and under other circumstances I might behave and think as they do.

For instance, I have long been turned off by narrow-minded, uncompromising religious bigots. On our crowded planet they frighten me with their extreme tribalistic mentality. Yet, under different conditions in my life, might not I have developed into such a personality?

Furthermore, I must confess that cocky, omniscient-behaving, domineering, manipulative, status-seeking individuals, of which college campuses seem to have more than their share, have tended to disgust and repel me. But if various stimuli, influences, and models in my life had been different, might not I have been such an individual? Trying to think this way has, at least, made such individuals more tolerable.

But what about the real rejects in our midst, Leon? What about the wretched and despised who live among us? Could this "moccasin formula" apply to them?

Could we say that there but for the grace of God go I when we think of cold-blooded murderers?

Could we say that there but for the grace of God go I when we think of avaricious individuals who would betray their country to make a few extra thousand dollars?

Could we say that there but for the grace of God go I when we think of rapists who violently harm innocent citizens?

103

Could we say that there but for the grace of God go I when we think of child molesters who attack young sons and daughters?

Could we say that there but for the grace of God go I when we think of the Oklahoma City bombers?

Are there not limits, Leon, on how far we can go in walking in another man's shoes? Are there not limits to the grace of God?

Or does God *really* love these people too?

Glory Be: The Personal In Life!

Several times recently I have remarked to friends that I would find teaching now much more difficult than I did when I was employed as a professor. I would not be nearly as certain of many theories, beliefs, schools of thought, and so on as I was when I was younger. The knowledge explosion is eroding old certitudes, perspectives, and frameworks of thought, Leon.

Yet at the same time that I find myself less certain of many of the beliefs I once had, other vistas of thought are emerging that more than offset the loss of former belief systems. Among these evolving thought patterns are my views of immortality. Unlike some of my colleagues, I never disavowed beliefs in immortality; I just never gave the subject a great deal of attention. I must acknowledge that to admit interest in this matter of immortality is considered rather beneath the level of mature intellectual concerns by many faculty members I have known.

I suspect that the reaction of many intellectuals has been shaped by the old "pie-in-the-sky" emphasis of much religion past and present. As a consequence of this juvenile emphasis, such individuals have rejected in a wholesale fashion any belief in immortality. I, too, have recoiled from the dramatic "fire and brimstone" versions of religion that endeavor to frighten individuals into accepting certain brands of religion in order to acquire eternal life. There is little, if any, of the love of God in this kind of preaching. But to reject the idea of immortality just because of the crude presentations of this kind of religious emphasis seems to me to be something like "throwing out the baby with the bath water"!

My recent interest in immortality is not merely that I have arrived in the senior citizen era of life, but also because I see now a relationship between the erosion in this belief and our impersonal, mass society. Leon, I wonder if there is not a connection of some kind between diminishing beliefs in immortality and the current dehumanization of life. Human individuals have been treated in a dehumanized manner for many centuries, but here at the end of the twentieth century there seems to be an intensification and proliferation of this practice. When humans are viewed and treated as inconsequential objects, a setting is created wherein serious attention to immortality is diminished.

Daily in the mass media accounts of genocide, brutal wars, gang slayings, senseless murder on the streets, and so forth are reported. Added to this is the manner in which we are viewed as mere consumer objects valuable only for bringing in greater returns for profit-obsessed organizations. Even in the thought of many contemporary writers there is reflected a viewpoint that demeans human life. Human individuals are looked upon as a mere, insignificant bubble of life that is barely noticeable in the infinite reaches of the cosmos. The life of an individual is at most a burst of energy that is quickly spent and then disappears. If there is immortality, it is no more than just one's infinitesimal contributions to the pooled knowledge and goodness that accumulates in the whole of humankind.

Such thinking and writing seem to reflect the kind of mass society, population-exploding species of which we are a part. Puny humans are buried under an avalanche of mounting billions of human creatures. We just don't count as individuals any more. Very definitely nothing is preserved beyond these earthly lives we so briefly live, according to this outlook, so it seems. "The killing fields" describe impersonal organisms being extinguished and the actuality of real, valuable human individuals becomes a receding myth.

Our little planet and any accomplishments we humans make upon this celestial body are probably nil in this vast universe that our scientists are finding out about. If we ever tended toward being haughty, arrogant individuals in our learning, we should have been humbled by the explorations, inventions, and almost incomprehensible reaches of knowledge that have been occurring in recent decades. In all of this the possibility of anything like a personal immortality seems almost ridiculous.

But, Leon, have we maybe overlooked another whole dimension of thought? Do any of us begin to come close to understanding the depths and intricacies of what *personal* may signify? We human beings are feeling, experiencing creations as well as thinking creatures, are we not? When we experience deep, growing, expanding love with another, is this just a passing pulsating sensation? The *qualitative* aspects of deep, shared love — is this only a perishable occurrence? Are we humans who can experience and share in something like this doomed to shed such miraculous unions once we exit from this earthly life? Is something that may be so unique and wonderful limited by our mortality, Leon?

I don't believe we humans have come very close yet to appreciating the kind of species we are. *We may be* considerably more unique in this universe than we begin to realize. The qualitative aspects of our lives that we have been unable to measure and explain successfully by the ordinary measurements of empirical science may be much more the identifying characteristics of ourselves than is recognized by the orthodox, scholarly thought of our time!

There is something marvelous, overwhelming, and personal, Leon, about how we humans are able to live and relate to others. Furthermore, for those who believe as I do, that there is a Divine indwelling in us, our human race is infinitely more complex and profound than we have begun to understand. I tend to suspect that we have only scratched the surface in trying to convey the truly unique features of humankind.

In this line of thought then, Leon, what has planted within us this urge to articulate hints of immortality that we sense from time to time? Poets, philosophers, theologians, and others sometimes have made efforts to set forth some expressions of this in their writings, but unlimited exploration and experiencing lie before us that only sporadic writing has touched upon. There seems to be good reason to believe that there is something here that does not perish. It is of a whole different strata of thought than what we commonly communicate to others. And what is involved here is very personal. Maybe our lives as we know them are merely on the threshold of a whole new realm of experience in which the glories of the personal will be revealed in the discoveries we encounter beyond this present existence. I tend to think this is a very real possibility, Leon!

A Die Hard?

Why are there people turned off by religion, Leon? Really, I wonder, would not the more appropriate question be, why are not more people turned off by religion than apparently there are? When one takes into account all the hate-filled, derogatory, insulting comments and writings made in the name of religion, it is no wonder, is it, that sensitive individuals are repelled? Then when one takes into account the past and present strife carried on in the name of religious truth, there is more reason than ever for those concerned with the welfare of humankind to reject religion.

Leon, I don't want to discard what might be called the religious element in life. My religious heritage has meant much to me. This recognition is not to ignore the fact, though, that there is much truth in all the great religions. No religion, in spite of what some zealous, blind followers believe, can claim any monopoly on truth, can it, Leon? Naturally, I am more aware of the beneficial influence for humanity of my own Judeo-Christian tradition, but I am aware, I hope, of some of the many virtues in other religious traditions as well.

Sometimes, though, would it not almost be helpful if we could eliminate the term "religion" from our vocabulary? Is it not spiritual nourishment and guidance that religions, at their best, are to contribute to our lives? If we think in terms of the spiritual condition and development of humans, and when so doing leave out referring to one's religion, perhaps we could avoid some of the negativism associated with the term.

When one considers the spiritual condition of individuals and groups of people, one may be able to come closer to understanding the many conflicting, confusing observations made about religion. Are not individuals and groups of people in various stages of spiritual development? An understanding of this subject is what writers like M. Scott Peck are endeavoring to help us with, I believe.

According to Peck, individuals exist in and may grow into various stages of spiritual life.*   Probably most people in our own culture whom we commonly think of as "religious" are in what Peck designates as the Stage II or "Formal, institutional" level of spiritual existence. These individuals find their security and sense of well-being in the identification they have with their particular religious group or institution. They are attached to the "forms" of their particular religion rather than the "essence" of their religion, as Peck describes the condition.

Consequently, if individuals in this Stage II of spiritual development believe the forms of their religion are being threatened, they can react in extremely hostile and even belligerent kinds of behavior. Individuals in what Peck refers to as other stages of spiritual development are often repelled, then, by these Stage II adherents. Furthermore, those in the Stage II classification feel threatened by those in stages of spiritual development more advanced than their own. So in addition to conflict among varied religious groups in Stage II development, there is strife often between the Stage II people and those in more advanced stages of spiritual development.

In despair, then, Leon, for the outside observer, the whole subject of religion seems to open up a picture of complexity and confusion that almost defies analysis and understanding. Would not a concentration on the social and psychological conditions influencing the spiritual life of humans avoid some of this confusion? I believe it might do so, and writers like Peck have made contributions to such an understanding.

Leon, I desire to be able to relate meaningfully to individuals in all walks of life, to people in all stages of spiritual development, to those with all kinds of belief. There have been times that I have thought this wish next to impossible with many humans. The dogmatism, the irrationality, the provincial mentalities of many, I have found extremely difficult to tolerate, let alone understand. Yes, I must admit, often I avoid such individuals. But I just can't surrender the belief, naive as perhaps it may be, that there is always the potential for meaningful communication with all humans. A foolish perspective? Some of my colleagues would say "yes."

I hope they are mistaken, Leon.

—————————

*Peck, M. Scott, *The Different Drum* (New York: Simon & Schuster, 1987), pp. 186-200.

Slow Learner

"Will you ever learn?" says one's spouse as one again engages in non-productive behavior. Perhaps a husband has again attempted to repair the engine on their automobile and has only succeeded in the car's performing more poorly. This is not the first time he has done something like this. He is a slow learner in realizing that there are many mechanical problems he cannot solve.

With me, Leon, it's being a slow spiritual learner. It seems that it takes a long time for the greater spiritual truths to soak in with me. For instance, I know that a quiet period of meditation each day can make a great difference in the way the day goes for me. But frequently in my hurried life I ignore this spiritual insight and then wonder why the day has been so hectic. Or in the heat of controversy I belatedly realize that my ego has been wounded and I have handled the situation poorly, when I should have known that if I had tried to understand more thoroughly the others with whom I was in conflict, I would not have been so centered on the welfare of my own ego and the outcome of the situation might have been more positive for us all.

Then one of the truths that I have learned very slowly, so it seems, is that security and lasting satisfaction does not come with the acquisition of possessions. Many times I have heard various versions of the folly of laying up for yourself "treasuries where moth and rust can creep in and destroy," and yet much of my life when I have been able to do so I have accumulated these treasuries way in excess of my basic needs. Clothes, tools, musical records, sports equipment, food, and building supplies have been among the items that I have excessively accumulated. The satisfactions that the original purchase of such items brought has just not lasted. And I think I really knew at the time of the purchase this would happen. How often can we keep deceiving ourselves by thinking that some purchases will even come close to bringing us lasting satisfaction?

Why are some of us such slow learners? Why can't we more fully understand early in our lives that a great truth such as love's ultimately conquering all does really have some validity to it? Is our problem due to ignorance? Stubbornness? Blindness? Perverseness? Shallowness? I am not sure what it really is. Although there are those who think they know the answer to this, I am not sure there is a satisfactory answer.

As a teacher, I know that it was always exciting to see some of the students who at the beginning of their college career appeared to be rather unpromising pupils later come to life and become very capable and bright learners. Is God One who experiences great satisfaction in observing us finally beginning to grow spiritually? If so, maybe there is some hope for us slow learners.

Strange World

*"The world dreams of things to come, and then
in due season arouses itself to
their realization."*
— Alfred North Whitehead

*Is there a shortage of "fuel" today,
Leon, for dreaming?*

I'm Right!

Leon, for how many individuals might the following soliloquy represent their thoughts and feelings?

"I know what I really believe.
I believe every word of the Bible is divinely inspired.
I believe there is only one true religion.
I believe that monogamy is the only right kind of marriage.
I believe that husbands should be the head of their households.
I believe that the only real family is one consisting of father, mother, and children.
I believe that the love of a man for a woman is the only acceptable kind of sexual orientation.
I believe that what has made America the greatest nation in the world is good, old-fashioned hard work and initiative by many individuals.
I believe that anyone can succeed if one tries enough.
I believe a free market is the only way a nation can achieve prosperity.
I believe that the only way to deal with the crime problem is to punish offenders more severely.
I believe that some races of people have greater intelligence than others.
I believe that human nature being what it is, there will always be wars.

"These beliefs I hold dearly. I will not accept any other views than these. No, I will not change my thoughts on these matters. No, I will not compromise my stand on these subjects. I am absolutely sure of myself.

"I shudder when I think of what some kinky people say. When I read and hear how other people live, I am upset. God, I know I'm right. God, don't let anyone know how uncomfortable I am living in this crazy world. I've just got to be right. I don't want to lose my 'cool.' I don't want my world to collapse around me."

In a world of great human diversity, just how dangerous is such thinking?

Provincial Revelry

Leon, when I meet individuals who have traveled widely, people who have met and known others of many religious faiths, people who have talked with and become acquainted with citizens from the far corners of the globe, people who have read broadly, people who have been unafraid to have their minds stretched, people who could be justifiably regarded as citizens of this world, I am uncomfortable. They tend to create an unease within me that some of my beliefs and perspectives might have some flaws. Consequently, I would like to return to the comfort and security of my "cocooned living" by ascribing to denials of the numerous challenges that contact with "world citizens" thrust upon me.

I would deny or ignore that people of other religious faiths believe their scriptures are as sacred and truth-rewarding as my own are for me.

I would deny or ignore that customs and lifestyles of respected individuals in other lands may be as comfortable for them as my own are for me.

I would deny or ignore that my own experiences are only a billionth of a drop of the experiences that humans have recorded.

I would deny or ignore that I can only make very tentative judgments about others based upon my very limited experiences.

I would deny or ignore that the carefully researched and painstaking work of scientific scholars and the theories they formulate based upon their studies, critically appraised by other scientists around the world, and subject to continual revisions, may be nearer the truth than the dogmas propounded by the leaders of my particular religious associations.

I would deny or ignore any tendency on my part and those who believe as I do to engage in warding off any doubts that may creep into my "security system" by resorting to name-calling and labeling in demeaning ways the thought of those who disturb me.

I would deny or ignore that I may wish to revel in the thought patterns of those I like and who think as I do.

Leon, I would glory in the fact that I just don't want to think. I don't want my cocoon invaded!

Innocence Regained?

Sometimes, Leon, my thoughts wander back to my childhood days when our family lived in a northern Illinois rural community. My father was the pastor of a village church to which the overwhelming majority of the residents of the community belonged. Nearly everyone knew one another, helped each other out when there was trouble, gathered together for community festivities, and on basic issues were more or less of one mind. I can picture sitting in the church on Sunday mornings as good old gospel songs were sung and sense something of the security and well-being that was diffused through the congregation.

There was little apparent division and conflict of ideas among these people, Leon. Problems and turmoil in Europe were light years away. Chicago, the nearest large city, in "mind miles" was a great distance removed. We lived in our little, peaceful community cushioned from the discord and uncertainties of the larger world way out there. In my mind, Leon, it is a picture in stark contrast to the violence, political wrangling, mass distortions, confusing diversity, and economic insecurity that pervade every part of our nation today. If someone could promise, with good reason, to offer the opportunity to return to the idyllic conditions my boyhood habitat seemed to possess, there are times that the urge to accept such a promise would be difficult to reject.

I, and others, grow weary coping with the increasing complexity, disorganization, and turbulence that engulf our country and our planet. Routes of escape from it that would seemingly assure a contrasting life of peace, accord, and good will among the inhabitants are most appealing. Can we be blamed for our plight?

But, Leon, is it really possible to return to the state of individual and collective innocence we think we once possessed? Can we really have the conveniences, contemporary amenities, diversified entertainment, standards of living, and so forth of today without paying a price for them? Can we accept the enticements of those religious and political leaders that appear in every nation who promise to lead us back to "Eden" without paying a terrific charge? Earlier in this century there were those Germans who thought their Fuhrer could restore their lost innocence, and look what happened. Do not these types of leaders constantly float among us who, in deceptive disguises, often in very cleverly devised, high-financed "packages," work upon our nostalgic yearning for a more innocent, simple, tranquil existence?

A number of years ago, Karl Popper cautioned and warned about the appeals and manipulations of those who would restore the orderly, undisturbed life many of us imagine existed once upon a time. As much as we may desire what seems to be turning the hands of the clock back to a much preferred kind of world of yesterday, such is impossible. As Popper asserts, *once innocence is lost it can never be regained!**

Is this true, Leon? Popper says the worries, the disorder, the competing values, the unsettledness of contemporary life is the price we pay for civilization. The way today we are forced, like it or not, to confront these conflicting appeals and make personal decisions in the midst of diversity is a part of being human. We cannot pretend to be creatures incapable of using our mentality constantly to evaluate the appeals for support among the many voices clamoring for our attention. Our full human potential is called into play today, is it not?

Scary? Perhaps! Challenging? An understatement! May my weariness never get the best of me!

---

*Popper, Karl R., *The Open Society and Its Enemies* (Princeton: Princeton University Press, 1950), pp. 165-195.

To The Scrap Pile

By Jupiter, how we need to get tough today!
Crime and immorality are sweeping our country.
All kinds of deviants are threatening our values.
Far too long have we coddled and tolerated the
perverts of our society.
Not any too soon are leaders finally beginning to stand up
to those influences that have allowed these destructive,
murderous forces to run wild.

Never mind, oh Jupiter, the fact that policies of the past
that stressed "get tough" practices never really worked.
Just let us dress up these dead-end strategies with modern
political/religious jargon and they should work.
Stifle the voices of the do-gooders.
To the scrap pile with their soft, deceiving, unrealistic
sentimentalities.
It's time we squarely faced the menace that confronts us.
By Jupiter, it really is time we get tough!

The only kind of language these outcasts understand is
brute force.
No signs of weakness or uncertainty must be shown.
Empathy, kindness, consideration, understanding, and
compassion are absolutely inappropriate.
These outlooks are the dribble of bleeding hearts!
In the rough and tumble of today, there is no place for
the failed counsel of rose-colored advocates.

By Jupiter, let's take off the soft gloves.
No more protecting and pampering these outlaws.
Make life as miserable as possible for their
incarcerations.

Make no effort to conceal the hatred toward them.
They're scum, treat them like scum.
Lock them up and really throw away the keys.
Excise them from our midst.
Listen. By Jupiter, we know how to deal with them.

Leon, *never, never, let me get aboard this popular bandwagon!*

Bitterness Fever

I hate Serbs for what they have done to my people.

I hate the Israelis for the bombings of my native Lebanon.

I hate the English for how they have treated my Irish brethren.

I hate Moslems for how they have tortured my Hindu kinfolk.

I hate Whites for the genocide of my Native American tribes.

I hate men for how they have dominated women.

I hate pro-choice individuals for how they condone abortions.

I hate "gays" for the perversions they commit.

I hate "liberals" for their softness on crime.

I hate gun-control advocates for their disregard for freedom.

I hate "rednecks" for the bigotry they perpetuate.

On could go the listing of the recital of hatreds so widespread throughout the world and our society. Oh, how much hatred and bitterness there is today, Leon. Has it ever been more intense and universal than it seems now? It is in the very air we breathe. It is a fever that infects us before we know what is happening to us.

What does this fever do to us? Does it not dissipate our creative energies? Does it not push us into "lumping" many innocent individuals into negative stereotypes? Does it not make us susceptible to the rhetoric of demagogic leaders who profit from heating up these racial, ethnic, and social hatreds? Does it not encourage finding scapegoats for our complex problems? Does it not fuel our most crass inclinations? Does it not drain us of what is humane about us?

This pervasive bitterness is like an aggressive cancer spreading through the social fabric, is it not? Is the situation hopeless? Sometimes it seems like it is. But is not much of this bitterness fever the work of the mass media? Do not the leaders in the mass media industry accept an assumption that human attention is much more easily gained and profits more readily assured by playing up accounts of human hatred and bitterness than by focusing upon love, good will, and civility? Do many of these media leaders seriously question such an assumption? Do these leaders, collectively, ever seriously try to change in creative ways the themes they publicize in their industry?

Many humans do rise above the legacy of hatred and bitterness they are born into, do they not? As is sometimes said, there are many unnoticed, unacclaimed "saints" amongst us, are there not, Leon? And when we stop to take note of them, most of us have known some of them, have we not?

Our Christian scriptures claim that the greatest force in the world is love, do they not, Leon? Dare we give this force a chance in our lives? Bitterness and hatred may be a fever, a cancer, threatening our individual and national lives, *but there is a cure*, is there not? May we never lose sight of this fact!

Really A Sham?

A high school teacher does not like to be bothered with the time consumed in grading essay tests, but tells his class that only multiple choice questions will be on their tests, for this kind of test best reveals how well they understand the subject matter of the course. Is the teacher engaged in a form of sham?

A stockbroker knows that certain groups of investments are very risky but tells his clients they are safe and a good buy. Is he engaged in what might be called sham?

A product is advertised as being capable of bringing youth and beauty to anyone who purchases it when the producers know very well that the ingredients of the product have absolutely no such effect. Is this sham, Leon?

Political leaders tell the public that some pending legislation will benefit everyone, knowing that this is not true and that the legislation will help only a privileged few. Is this not sham, Leon?

The anthropologist Jules Henry once presented a paper at a Conference on Society and Psychosis in which he pointed out that life today is more or less one great sham. Few, if any of us, escape from giving false information to others. Reality is so often distorted that what is *reality* becomes more than an academic question. The world we humans seem to be creating is a fake world, according to Henry.

Is this so? There are times that I fear I would tend to agree with him. Lies, distortions, deceptions, and misrepresentations seem to be the rule of the day. Who can be trusted? Are we humans, Leon, immersed in an existence of tragic proportions? I hope such a picture of contemporary life is overdrawn, but sometimes I wonder if there is not considerable accuracy to such an analysis.

In the conclusion of his paper, Henry states that we can respond to sham in three ways: (1) believe sham to be the truth; (2) see through sham while using it; (3) see through sham but fight it. He further writes that these ways of dealing with sham constitute stages of social evolution through which humankind is passing. Finally, he adds a fourth stage to these which can be envisioned, namely, "a world without sham."*

Leon, let others and me strive diligently for a world without sham!

---

*Henry, Jules, "Sham," in *On Sham, Vulnerability and Other Forms of Self-Destruction* (New York: Vintage Books, 1973), pp. 126-127.

No-Win

There is a witticism that goes, "Why do we buy things we don't want, just to impress people we can't stand the sight of?" Disturbingly, I fear, there is some truth in this witticism, isn't there, Leon? The urge to impress others with our importance motivates us into what is really irrational behavior. In fact, the behavior is often humorous when one views it from an outside perspective! How many of us at times have dragged home grotesque purchases because we at first thought they would be impressive objects to have around our homes? They probably were impressive, but not in the way we hoped they would be!

I would tend to think most of us are not fully aware of what we are doing in this kind of activity. In fact, if we could in some way calculate what percentage of our expenditures was consumed in the selection of purchases that essentially served our subconscious desire to impress others, we would be shocked with the findings! The sale of smelling salts would skyrocket! I recall some years ago when I purchased a new automobile that was our first higher status car. I remember how the prestigious emblem on this more expensive automobile caught my attention and subconsciously I thought others would take note of this new car when we drove up in front of their homes. I am sure it was debatable if the quality of this car was particularly superior to less expensive ones. But my, how striking this car appeared to me — especially as I thought I saw it through the eyes of others!

If I scratched deeply enough into my subconscious, I suspect that I would recall many similar incidents where I was buying to impress others. Yet we are reluctant to admit that such motivations play a part in our consumership. This kind of acquisition is a silent game for most of us; in varying degrees of skill we play this game of deceiving ourselves and others about what we are really doing.

One version of this silent game we popularly refer to as "keeping up with the Joneses." We feel our self-images are diminished if we appear to be falling behind in possessing goods owned by others important to us. If they purchase more expensive cars, we soon try to do the same. If they make it known they have acquired a luxury boat, we will soon endeavor to possess one. If they move into a more prestigious neighborhood, we will likely attempt to do likewise. And the game goes on and on.

We tend to think our worth, as well as the worth of others, is equated with how successfully we are able to participate in this silent game. The game extends into many areas of our lives. Even as parents of grown children, we make known to friends, in one way or another, that our children have been given a job promotion, that they have purchased a new home, that they have taken a cruise in the Caribbean, that they have joined a prestigious club. We want others to know our children are worth something and that they, too, are succeeding in this silent game. We are embarrassed and uncomfortable if we have to indicate our children appear to be unsuccessful in this activity.

In many insidious ways, I fear, does this game absorb our time, energy, and resources. Yet, do we ever win, Leon? If we do supposedly get ahead of those with whom we have been associating, don't we move into another level of players who are engaged in the same behavior, albeit perhaps more expensive, more artfully carried out, and so on? Caught up in this kind of silent game, do we ever stop to think that we will always encounter others who have a little more of whatever our "set" is valuing, something a little better, something more novel?

Is this living, real living, or is it a supercilious, ultimately self-destructive, degrading game in which our real human worth is measured in false terms and we are reduced to some kind of automatons pushed and pulled by the fashion setters, the advertisers, the acquisitive, and the ridiculous? Do we dare probe the underlying motivations present in much of our consuming behavior, Leon?

Dare We?

May it be that we are blind today, Leon? Is not the thinking of most of us locked in to thinking of national states as the ultimate in political units? In the post-World War II era have not Western leaders proceeded blindly to encourage and assist in the birth of new nation-states, thereby repeating and imitating Western powers in guarding their sovereignties? One end result of this might then be spreading the dangers of conflict on an increasingly crowded planet.

Not only in regard to political units is the thinking of many of us limited in scope, but in other ways as well. Our cultures and limited experiences confine our mentalities. Few individuals seriously question deeply ingrained cultural values. An example of this is our acceptance in the Western world of the idea of *profit*. Few dare openly, Leon, question the assumption that what exchanges among individuals and organizations are ultimately done bring profit to the parties involved. Our economic system, which for many individuals appears to be their religion, rests upon the concept of profit, doesn't it, Leon? We dress up our references to our economic system, don't we, by calling it "free enterprise"?

But dare we question the ethical, individual, and social consequences of this foundation of thought? If we did, Leon, what might be some of the discomforting disclosures we might uncover? Would our conclusion possibly be that many of the ills in our world today can finally be reduced to *greed*? Would we, furthermore, note that *greed* is generously mixed in with the idea of *profit*? Would we perhaps note that much of the distorted news we receive through the media is the result of the ownership of these news sources emphasizing profit over accurate news reporting? Would we observe that the corruption in our political and business world boils down to profit-seeking? Would we find even with many charitable organizations that showing a profit on their books is more important to them than needed services to their clients? Would we

129

see, through the lies, that much of what advertising reduces to is predicated on increasing profits? Would we even disturbingly find that many of our relationships with others, including those we are purported to love, are characterized by an element of profit? Don't we all too often expect our ties with others ultimately to be profitable for us?

Even when we claim that making profit is necessary in order to acquire the means to provide services for others, would we find buried rationalizations present if we probed deeply enough? Do the ends justify the means if we dare really to think through what may be at work here, Leon?

Dare we entertain the thought that profit may be one of the most insidious social problems affecting our world? Is it heresy to think this way? Dare we relate the implications of the biblical passage, "For what shall it profit a man if he gains the whole world and loses his own soul"* to the ultimate futility of profit-seeking? Doesn't the very concept of profit, brutally and honestly confronted, usually mean that someone is gaining at another's expense? Are we a part of some kind of social "ice age" in which our minds and actions are frozen by a kind of accepted living that is more and more paralyzing us as a species with its destructive consequences?

It scares me, Leon.

---

*Mark 8:36 KJV

Novelty Addiction

My six-year-old granddaughter says she is bored. Parents of our grandchildren frequently refer to their children as being bored. Leon, "bored" is a word that was absent in my vocabulary when I was growing up. No doubt I was bored at times, but I did not know it!

What is happening to the present generation of youth? Many American children are surrounded by more toys, playthings, luxuries, and so on than past generations ever dreamed of having. Yet they are often bored. What does this say about us, Leon?

Could part of the condition be that life today for many of us has been saturated with so many different possessions, varied experiences, and rapid changes that we keep wanting new and different toys, new and different television programs, new surroundings, new and more novel adventures? Behavioral scientists have pointed out that one of the basic drives or wishes for humans is new experience. Could it be that early in life we have been exposed to such a range of new experiences that we find it increasingly difficult to find something really new and different to consume in the way of a new experience as we grow on into adulthood? Are we victims of novelty addiction?

It is frightening to think what could happen to many of us if novelty addiction should intensify. What kind of bizarre toys, sports, mass media programs, and so forth may the future hold? Can we humans in generations to come ever be content again with simple pleasures? Will we finally reach a stage of such restlessness that in one final act of desperation we destroy ourselves in a fitful unleashing of our weapons of mass destruction? Leon, perish such thoughts! Yet the continued flooding of our markets with new and novel products does raise disturbing questions about the psychological, social, and spiritual effects of this "feeding" of our appetite.

With many of us, where is any awareness of our own internal, spiritual resources? Are we dependent entirely upon external stimuli to find new zest in our living? Have we early in our lives allowed these inner qualities to atrophy so that we only respond to the parade of novelties placed before us by contemporary hucksters?

One cannot help but suspect, can one, that a bored people are potentially dangerous? Could it not be that they are easily susceptible to demagogic leaders who promise to bring novelty and excitement into their lives? Cannot gang leaders, charismatic religious and political leaders, and obsessed messiahs prey upon the discontents of bored individuals?*

The more I think about it, Leon, we need to devote more attention to antidotes for this novelty addiction. I fear the situation could really get out of hand!

———————————

*Could it be that contemporary extremist groups such as what we refer to as "skinheads" might, at least partly, be understood in this context of novelty addiction?

Deadlock

A popular book two generations ago was the Republican presidential candidate Wendell Willkie's *One World.* Back then there was an awakening to the need to be aware of how our world was, indeed, becoming one world with modern mass transportation, communication, and commerce. Groups like the World Federalists, Union Now, and others were working to bring about greater political and economic unification of nations. Today the presence of multinational corporations as world wide phenomena are just taken for granted in many influential circles. Even with its shortcomings, the United Nations is an accepted necessity by most informed people.

Yet the visions of an integrated world inspired by such books as Willkie's seem rather anemic. Leon, few of us have minds that conceptualize in global terms. Our ultimate identity is with our nation-state, and as is all too obvious, in our thinking and actions we support our nations' needs at the expense of the rest of the world. Elected political leaders would not dare publicly advocate global needs at the expense of their own nation's well-being. But in view of the trends, wished for or not, toward world interdependency, are most of our leaders and their followers anachronistic creatures?

We seem to lack the mental pictures, the mythology, as one like Joseph Campbell would describe the matter, to assist us in grasping this emerging world of which we are a part. This seems strange, Leon, for the world religions give little, if any, credence to the ultimate importance of nation-states. They project global and universal images. Most of us seem to proceed, nevertheless, to ignore these religious implications.

Furthermore, with all the zeal of post-war youth in many parts of the world to find worthy missions to pursue and promote, the greatest energies seem to have been consumed with provincial, parochial endeavors. One would have thought by now that some

133

inspiring, visionary leaders would have emerged who could captivate idealistic youth into a crusade to implement the ideals of one like Wendell Willkie. Instead, in every nation and ethnic group, leaders keep emerging who excite youthful energies toward what amounts to tribal goals. Nothing seems to stir up the emotions and enthusiasm of individuals like historic appeals to their ethnic and national identities. What kind of mental blockage has been occurring here, Leon?

Wise people around the world know that our fragile planet, our endangered human species, cannot long continue to exist in the fragmented condition in which we find ourselves. But we, for the most part, seem paralyzed in being able to do anything effective in countering this fragmentation. If our species must soon perish, Leon, how much better would it be if we perished in ignorance? But, Leon, are most of our leaders really as naive and ignorant about our ethnic and national blindness as they appear to be? I wonder.

Oh, that we would break the kind of mental-emotional deadlock in which we seem to be mired at the moment! Leon, humankind just has to have visionary, truly realistic leaders who can communicate with the masses about our present ethnic, national follies. *Is the only other option one in which the world must experience an unprecedented calamity before we come to our senses?* God forbid! God have mercy!

Some Concluding Grazing

*"He who knows the world as something by which he
is to profit knows God also in the same way. His
prayer is a procedure of exoneration heard by
the ear of the void. He — not the 'atheist,' who
addressed the Nameless out of the night and
yearning of his garret window — is the
godless man."*
— Martin Buber

*Leon, is the desire for that "peace which
passes all understanding" compatible
with the yearning, the seeking of
the Divine Presence?*

Can't Help It!

Leon, what drives me down here to my study at five o'clock in the morning? Hasn't the writing of these questions, these "grazings," these ponderings gotten out of hand?

Leon, I'm not a young man. I need more rest. Why do I have to write when silent conversation with you is brewing? Why can't these moments be arranged at more convenient times?

Am I sort of what some might say possessed? I don't want to view myself or have others consider me "too far off center"!

Is my ego so hungry that I really want recognition from these writings? You know what I think about those whom I know and have met with poorly disguised monstrous egos. I don't want to be shoved into such a classification!

Leon, although I may complain at times about the social isolation of this beautiful retirement home, you know I really love it here. I like the peace and quiet that surrounds us. I cherish the daily manifestations of nature and the intriguing antics of its forested creatures. I would resent having this all disturbed by ramifications of this writing.

But I can't seem to help myself, Leon. I just have to set these grazings, ponderings, and questions into printed word.

I love my country and I hate to see it being threatened with manipulative, self-seeking, greedy, short-sighted leaders. I am troubled with the way the defenseless, the "publicans" of our age, are shoved around like pawns on a giant chess board. My religious heritage tells me to speak out for them.

I love this planet on which we humans dwell. I feel something very moving when astronauts relate their feelings about the beauty that this blue-colored celestial sphere has upon them. When they look down upon it, they see no national boundaries, no ethnic groupings, no divisions. They just see a striking, awe-inspiring heavenly body hurling through space. I want to help preserve its beauty and its wonders. I just can't keep silent when tribalistic leaders think solely in terms of what they call national interests and don't care how these interests may impact upon the rest of the world.

I don't like to listen to much of the news reporting, Leon. Most of it seems to focus upon violent and hate-driven events and individuals. Sometimes, I cowardly turn it off. There is not much love among us humans revealed in these newscasts. I guess it is not sensational enough. Reporters telling about the many incidents of love they could observe among us would be looked upon as naive, overly sentimental, and peculiar individuals. Yet there is so much good that permeates our collective life and so much more that could be encouraged by dedicated, selfless leadership. I just have to do what little I can, Leon, to help create more good and decency among us. I'm not afraid to be called a "do-gooder," am I, Leon?

What drives me down here to my study? I guess there are many factors involved here. I hope not too many of them are hidden forms of ego gratification. If so, surely there must be easier paths to pursue for such pleasures. I don't want to fool myself or others, Leon. I just know that in recent months, I have to write what is written here. Whatever the reasons, whatever discomforts may be encountered, whatever the consequences, I believe it is worth it!

Seeking

Truth sought and found. Truth elusive. Truth is relative. Truth is an illusion. Truth monopolies. Truth revealed. Truth seeker. Truth once and for all. Thoughts and statements about truth could be extended almost indefinitely, could they not, Leon? Philosophers, theologians, and seers have long asked, "What is truth?" What is one to believe about truth?

In a profound, consuming sense, I fear that I am not aware of having been very often disturbed by the question, "What is truth?" In a lighter, more pragmatic vein of thought, I have frequently raised the question to myself and others, where can one find truth about the reporting of current events? Like many people today, I am disturbed with news sources and am suspicious that they are distorting the truth in their reporting. But this certainly is not the fundamental question that inquiring, searching, penetrating minds have been raising about truth.

I guess I tend to come at the ultimate question concerning truth through the "side door"! That is to say that this question usually comes to the forefront of my thinking when I come across individuals who claim *they have the truth.* They know what the final truth is and brandish the appearance of having no doubts about this. Then my mental, spiritual, and psychological processes stir into action. I usually refrain, I fear, from openly expressing my reactions to these individuals, but inwardly these processes are at work!

How presumptuous, how self-deluding, how arrogant can individuals be, Leon? How can anyone claim to have the full, final truth when the wisest minds of the ages have searched and continue to search for the truth? What kind of inner insecurities are such people really trying to cover up? Depending on the particular individual, I vary in my reactions by feeling pity, sorrow, disgust, anger, and contempt for such claims to ultimate truth.

Yet we humans do feel the need for some kind of assurance, some kind of security, some kind of guiding star for our living, do we not? Most of us do want some values, some beliefs, some assumptions that we can rely upon for providing meaning and direction to our lives, do we not, Leon? Does this mean, though, that we have to have some kind of final truth? I believe not.

Sometimes I used to point out in my classes that we overlook what it would be like if any of us ever finally reached the ultimate truth. What would life be like for us then? Where would further adventure and exploration in the world of ideas then occur for us? What would happen to our mental zest? What would be the impact upon us for any scientific impulses we might possess when the drive for new truths no longer exists?

After raising questions like these, Leon, I would proceed with my students to point out that the search for truth may be like ever finding new, exciting rooms in a mansion, whereby you open one door into a room, only to find there are more doors beyond to open that can lead to additional discoveries and amazement. In other words, life is really basically adventurous and exciting, isn't it, Leon? If an individual definitely believes one has the final truth, does this not perhaps suggest a dull person? I hate to say this, but I wonder if something like this may not be the case.

Another thought occurs to me in regard to the subject of truth. Somewhere along the way, many of us have acquired the idea that to have any doubts about basic beliefs, especially what we regard as religious beliefs and dogmas, is to indicate a weakness and flaw in our character. Doubts are looked upon as sort of a small break in the protective dikes of our belief systems that threaten their very existence, so it seems. Yet is not a doubting perspective, Leon, more akin to a religious outlook than we may at first recognize? For isn't it by doubting and questioning that we either discard weak, unfounded beliefs or strengthen the ones that survive such examinations? Isn't an underlying trust present here that deeply held beliefs can be refined, strengthened, and made more meaningful by the doubting process?

Leon, I have to say that I am uncomfortable in the company of those who believe and claim they have a special hold on the truth and anyone who thinks otherwise is wrong, wicked, unsaved, despoiled, misled, or in some such fallen state of existence. I am uncomfortable with them because I strongly suspect they are self-deceiving, intolerant, or even that they are manipulative and endeavoring to influence others for self-serving motivations. Simply putting it, such truth-monopolizing persons turn me off! My negative reactions to them disturb me at times, and I must admit it is difficult for me to try to understand the most arrogant of these types of individuals. I fear I wish they would all migrate to some far, remote island! I know I need to work on this attitude, but this is how I often feel about them.

The company in which I find comfort and ease, Leon, is those who continue to seek. People who are willing to open their minds, people who are unafraid of laying aside pretensions, people who reveal their humility in the sight of God's magnificent, ongoing creations — ah, these are people who attract me. Are not such people truly alive, receptive, and sensitive to the unlimited marvels of this universe in which we live? Unapologetically, I would travel in this company.

"The Mysterium Tremendum"?

Early on, Leon, selecting sociology as a major area of study presented me with indications that my intellectual, spiritual journey would be different from many of my peers. This area of study combined with work at a young age as a juvenile court probation officer and later as a superintendent of a juvenile detention home steered me into what I guess one might call some unorthodox fields of interest and activity. At least, I am sure many of my acquaintances and family friends looked upon my thought and new fields of inquiry in this manner.

One example of my heading in directions not usually pursued by my peers was when I turned down a generous scholarship for my seminary studies in order that I could work full-time as a probation officer with the Polk County Juvenile Court in Des Moines, Iowa. Individuals offered such a scholarship just didn't do this! Later I recall in one of my seminary classes a discussion was under way among students and instructor concerning the kind of churches to build in the more affluent areas of our metropolitan communities. After the discussion had been rigorously pursued for a while, I raised my hand and asked, "What kind of churches are we to build in the poverty-stricken areas of our cities?" There was an awkward pause in the conversation and no direct response ensued. The discussion turned to other topics!

Yes, in a way one might say I was headed for trouble. My studies and my interests pointed me toward having to experience the tensions of what has been called the *marginal man*. I was destined to be somewhat unacceptable in subcultures with which I was associated. My interests and feelings for religion made me suspect among sociologists, who in the early postwar period tended to dismiss religion as more or less of an anachronism, and my identification as a sociologist made me a questionable individual among church leaders. In those earlier days of my vocational life, I really didn't have a spiritual home. The plight of a *marginal man* has somewhat pursued me to this day!

Yes, Leon, to be honest, I would say that I have missed having a spiritual home. But on the other hand, I would not, for the most part, wish that my life "gestalt" would have been greatly different. I knew, to a certain extent, what I was getting into when I made these choices. At the risk of sounding smug, and I certainly don't mean it that way, I have no major regrets. My life has had its share of ups and downs. My hedonistic inclinations would have avoided the more distressing moments had I been able to control outer and inner forces affecting me, but what of any significance would have been gained?

No, Leon, I suspect that some of us have to experience what might be called some trauma in order to glimpse that "beatific enjoyment of the Divine." "Smooth sailing" all the time does not contribute to much searching, does it?

Certainly, in my spiritual journey, through all of this, I am greatly indebted to numerous friends and inspiring teachers. These people in my life have been unassuming, unpretentious individuals who have quietly shared their mental and spiritual insights. I really am a most fortunate individual, Leon, to have had and to have such people in my life.

One of the most important mentors in my life, Leon, was Howard E. Jensen of Duke University. In a small advanced graduate class, I well remember how this seminar would frequently run an hour or more overtime in the late afternoon as he patiently answered our questions and unstintingly shared with us some of his most profound experiences and insights. No tuition could begin to cover what he did for us.

Upon Dr. Jensen's death, one of his colleagues wrote this in the closing paragraph of a memoriam to him: "Howard Jensen was deeply religious but he was not interested in religious politics. Like Par Lagerkvist's Ahasuerus, he sought the stupendous, inaccessible essence behind all the theologies, the rituals, the beliefs. He liked to quote the words of the dying Ahasuerus: 'Beyond the sacred clutter, the holy thing itself must exist. That I believe in.' "*

Leon, I hope and believe some of what Howard Jensen believed has permeated my life. If it has, I am the richer person for it!

---

*Thompson, Edgar T., "Howard Eikenberry Jensen, 1889-1970," in *The American Sociologist*, February 1971, p. 49.

Postscript

Originally I had not planned upon adding this note, but after further thought about the matter I thought it would be appropriate to write this. "Leon" is the name given to the anonymous spiritual guide in this writing. But the name does have a special significance for me and that is why I chose it to give to this guide. Leon was the name of my young brother who died just a few months before I was born. I have tended to consider myself a sensitive individual, but only in recent years have I more fully realized the impact this premature death had upon my family. Sensitivity is a lifelong matter of growth. I only wish I had sensed more how his death had influenced my parents and other members of my family when they were living. Thinking of a name, then, to give to the projected image of this spiritual counselor, I chose "Leon" to honor his influence upon us. Having said this, I should add that the choice was only to extend this recognition. No sense of communing with a deceased brother ever occurred to me as I was engaged in the writings which compose this publication.

Selected Bibliography

Allport, Gordon W., *The Individual and His Religion* (New York: The Macmillan Company, 1950).

Berger, Peter L., *Facing Up to Modernity* (New York: Basic Books, Inc., 1977).

Bonhoeffer, Dietrich, *Letters and Papers from Prison* (New York: The Macmillan Company, 1953).

Borysenko, Joan, *Minding the Body, Mending the Mind* (New York: Bantam Books, 1988).

Buber, Martin, *I and Thou,* second edition (New York: Charles Scribner's Sons, 1958).

Campbell, Joseph, *The Power of Myth* (New York: Anchor Books, 1991).

Dubos, Rene, *Beast or Angel? Choices That Make Us Human* (New York: Charles Scribner's Sons, 1974).

Eiseley, Loren, *The Firmament of Time* (New York: Atheneum Publishers, 1975).

Fox, Matthew, *Original Blessing* (Santa Fe: Bear & Company Publishers, 1983).

Harris, Sydney J., *Pieces of Eight* (Boston: Houghton Mifflin Company, 1982).

Henry, Jules, *On Sham, Vulnerability and Other Forms of Self-Destruction* (New York: Vintage Books, 1973).

Kelly, Thomas R., *A Testament of Devotion* (New York: Harper & Brothers Publishers, 1941).

Keyes, Ralph, *Timelock* (New York: Harper Collins Publishers, 1991).

Merton, Thomas, *Love and Living*, edited by Naomi Burton Stone and Brother Patrick Hart (New York: Bantam Books, 1979).

Mills, C. Wright, *The Sociological Imagination* (New York: Oxford University Press, 1956).

Montagu, Ashley, *Growing Young* (New York: McGraw-Hill Book Company, 1981).

Otto, Rudolf, *The Idea of The Holy*, translated by J. W. Harvey (New York: Oxford University Press, 1950).

Peck, M. Scott, *The Different Drum* (New York: Simon & Schuster, 1987).

Popper, Karl R., *The Open Society and Its Enemies* (Princeton: Princeton University Press, 1950).

Trueblood, Elton, *The Humor of Christ* (New York: Harper & Row Publishers, 1964).

Whitehead, Alfred North, *Adventures of Ideas* (New York: The Macmillan Company, 1933).